Candles
and
Candlecrafting

Candles
and
Candlecrafting

by Stanley Leinwoll

CHARLES SCRIBNER'S SONS NEW YORK

Printed in the United States of America
Library of Congress Catalog Card Number 72-6556
SBN 684-13187-0

TO MIRIAM, LAURA, AND JOAN

Acknowledgments

Many people and organizations helped make this book a reality. To list them all would be impossible. I am especially indebted to Mr. Charles M. Stern for the fine drawings, and to Miss Tanya Estrovich for many of the photos. I am grateful to Roger Railton-Jones of Carl Byoir and Associates who obtained for me material and information about the attractive line of candles by Hallmark Cards, Inc. Tony Kreutzer of Emkay Candle Company was very generous in allowing us to use his beautiful photos. We also wish to express our appreciation to the A. I. Root Company, Will and Baumer Candle Company, Gurley Candle Company, and Michelle Frager of Ruder and Finn, for the materials they supplied.

The American Handicrafts Company of Fort Worth, Texas, provided much useful information and photos of their line of candlecrafting products; Don Olsen, of the Pourette Manufacturing Company of Seattle, Washington, was a tremendous help in making available data dealing with the complete line of candle-making supplies his company markets.

Finally, I am especially indebted to my wife, Miriam, who spent long hours going over various drafts of the manuscript, making comments and suggestions which resulted in a much improved book.

Contents

Foreword

My first attempt at candlemaking was a total disaster. I had always been interested in candles, and when my sixth-grade daughter brought home a candle she had poured in a milk container during an arts-and-crafts class, I was fascinated, and decided to duplicate her effort.

I purchased several pounds of candle wax, wicking, and dye in a local hobby shop, "borrowed" my wife's double boiler, emptied a milk container found in our refrigerator, and proceeded eagerly.

I melted the wax in the top of the double boiler, "borrowed" a measuring cup, and began to pour the molten wax into the milk container.

What I did not know at the time, and what my daughter had neglected to tell me, was that the seams of milk containers are sealed with wax, and that heat can loosen the seal.

I had just realized that I had forgotten to put the wick in, when another, more immediate, problem arose: the seal at the bottom of the milk carton came apart, and hot wax was oozing out of it like molten lava.

The sight of the wax seeping slowly over the stove burners, into kitchen drawers, and onto the floor, caused me to panic. When I panic, I freeze, so I stood helplessly watching a quart of hot wax dribbling over everything in sight. Besides, what could one do to stop the flow?

My daughter found all of this very amusing. My wife did not. It took me three hours to clean up the mess.

If I had known what to do, the entire episode could have been prevented; it would have taken two minutes to secure the container with masking tape or rubber bands.

I have made many candles and many mistakes since that first ordeal ten years ago. The skyscraper candle pictured in this book is an original creation which has had considerable commercial success. It is a difficult candle to make, and I learned a great deal on the way to its development.

I frequently wished, along the way, that a book or books were available that could help me; that would teach about the properties of wax, wick, dyes, molds, techniques, etc.; that would give step-by-step detailed instructions for candlemaking. I found that what was available did not explain clearly what candles and candlemaking are all about.

This book is intended to remedy that situation. It will serve equally well for the novice who, like myself a decade ago, has never poured a candle but would like to do so, or for the experienced candlecrafter, who wishes to know more about the properties of paraffin, of the different dyes available, about additives, and about techniques with which he may not be familiar. The book is written simply and clearly, with ample illustrations to guide the reader.

With the general availability of all kinds of candlecrafting materials, there is virtually no limit to the variety of candles that can be produced by the home craftsman. In addition to the basic techniques of candlecrafting, this book will describe methods of making all the most popular types, including chunks, sand-casts, ice-cube candles, and many others.

Anyone can pour a candle, but doing it successfully requires know-how. There is a great feeling of accomplishment from taking a piece of wax and a length of wick and transforming it into an object of beauty. The reader will find everything he needs for successful candlecrafting in this book.

Gook luck!

Introduction

During the past decade the number of candles made and sold in the United States has more than doubled, and indications are that this trend will continue. Furthermore, foreign candle sales are showing similar increases.

To account for the phenomenal rise of interest in candles one need only visit a candle shop or department store where candles are sold. In contrast to the limited assortment of tapers and cylinders of fifteen years ago, today's candles are available in a mind-boggling range of shapes, sizes, and colors.

There are candles that resemble fruits, vegetables, birds, fish, animals, toys, and bottles; they can be multicolored or striped; they can spell "mom" or "dad"; there are "Peanuts" candles, and candles for all seasons of the year: Santa Claus for Christmas, turkeys for Thanksgiving, hearts for St. Valentine's Day, flowers for Easter, and red, white, and blue candles for the Fourth of

"Peanuts" candles and candlesticks have contributed to the great interest in candles during the past ten years. Courtesy Hallmark Cards, Inc.

For thousands of years candles have been burned for spiritual symbolism in religious services. Religious candles are as popular today as they have ever been. Courtesy Will and Baumer Candle Co., Inc.

The wise old owl can be hand-crafted at home from a rubber mold available commercially. Courtesy American Handicrafts Co.

July. There are Grecian urns, Venuses, and Madonnas, candles with multiple wicks, and candles three feet tall.

So rapidly has the industry expanded that the dictionary definition has become obsolete. A recent edition of *The American College Dictionary*, for example, defines a candle as "a long, usually slender, piece of tallow, wax, etc., with an embedded wick, burned to give light."

Candles do more than just provide light, much more: in literature and art the bright warm glow of candlelight has been a symbol of beauty, faith, joy, and enlightenment. For thousands of years candles have been burned for spiritual comfort in re-

14

Decorative animal candles are among the wide variety available today.
Courtesy Hallmark Cards, Inc.

ligious services, and the use of candles plays a prominent role in Protestant, Roman Catholic, and Jewish observances. The mood created by a subtly scented candle, burning in a darkened room, cannot be duplicated. Exotic candles are now used decoratively in all parts of the house as part of the decor. Candles are also used for the heat they provide, as, for example, under a chafiing dish.

The variety of candles is seemingly endless, and scarcely a week goes by that another new and original design does not reach some dealer's shelves.

And amazingly, most of these are priced under $5.00 each. As a result, people from all walks of life can afford to buy and enjoy candles; to use them decoratively, as conversation pieces, or to burn them.

Candles are reasonable in price for a number of reasons. The basic ingredient of candles, paraffin wax, is inexpensive. The price of a pound of paraffin varies according to location and the quantity purchased, but on the average it can be purchased at retail for under fifty cents per pound.

Competition is another factor. During the past generation leisure time in the United States increased significantly as work weeks shortened. Hobby industries grew as a result, and candlemaking as a creative art attracted increasing numbers of people. Candles are relatively easy to make in the home, and in addition to being low in cost, the materials are generally reusable. Unlike oil paints and some plastics, candle wax can be melted down and used again if a first attempt is unsuccessful.

Many home candlecrafters sell their surplus creations to candle shops and department stores. There are probably more people earning money from home candlecrafting than from any other home hobby. Because of this, competition is keen, and the cost of candles has remained moderate.

The availability of candlemaking materials has been a factor in the growth of home candle manufacture. Craft shops began to carry wax, wicking, scent, and low-cost metal molds. From a few basic mold shapes, the mold-making industry has boomed. One supplier of craft and hobby materials, The American Handicrafts Company, offers some forty-five different candle molds, in metal, plastic, and rubber. The Pourette Manufacturing Co. of Seattle, Washington, carries over 150 different molds. Anything from stars and cylinders to animals and exotic figures can be purchased. The company also supplies mold-making materials, which have revolutionized the candlemaking industry.

Synthetic liquid rubber is now readily available to anyone interested in making his own mold. This material sets in twenty-four hours, after which it is ready to use. Thus the imaginative hobbyist can create his own design, make a mold in a day, and begin producing candles a short time afterward.

The chemical industry has also contributed to candle sales; a wide range of chemical scents has been developed to add to the mood created by the charm of candle light. These include spice, gardenia, lilac, pine, bayberry, hyacinth, orange, lime, lavender, myrrh, frankincense, and many others.

The youth of the country has accounted, in part, for the current surge in candle sales; their increasing freedom, informality, and casual dress are part of an overall pattern toward a simpler life-style. The bright glow and soft beauty of candlelight suggest peace, freedom, faith, and serenity to the young. In addition the use of the candle, rather than electricity, symbolizes to an extent a rejection of modern technology.

Apart from producing candles for the pleasure of burning them, the young have taken to making candles as a means of earning money. Their new freedom has influenced their designs, further revolutionizing the industry. They have developed a variety of free forms, such as sand-cast candles, which are sculptures in addition to being candles; they have been innovators in producing psychedelic forms and color combinations, as well as new chunk-candle configurations.

It is evident from the foregoing that a combination of factors has been responsible for the phenomenal growth of interest in candles during the past decade. Foremost among these is the great variety available, and the ease with which candles can be made in the home.

History

Little is known of the origin of candles. It is believed that the first candles were developed by the ancient Egyptians from rushlights, which were made by soaking the pithy core of rushes, reeds, or grasses in molten tallow, obtained from cattle or sheep suet.

Subsequently, taper candles were developed by repeatedly dipping a fibrous wick into liquid tallow, which was allowed to cool and solidify between dippings until a desired thickness had been reached.

Cone-shaped candles in dishlike holders are depicted in relief on Egyptian tombs at Thebes, and a candleholder with a central socket found on the island of Crete in the Mediterranean was a product of the first Minoan civilization 5,000 years ago.

The Greeks and Romans used candles; a fragment of a tallow candle dating from the first century A.D. was found near Avignon, in France.

Tallow remained the principal ingredient of candles until the

Statuette of a youth in Persian costume: the support of a candelabrum. Greek, c. 450-400 B.C. The Metropolitan Museum of Art, Fletcher Fund, 1927.

Middle Ages, when beeswax—a substance secreted by honey bees to make their honeycombs—came into use. Beeswax candles were made by pouring the melted wax over a cotton wick, allowing it to cool, then repeating the process, which was continued until the candle was about an inch in diameter. It was then rolled over a hard surface to smoothen it.

Beeswax candles were a decided improvement over those made from tallow because the latter produced a smoky flame and emitted an acrid odor when burned. Beeswax candles, on the other hand, burned clean and pure. They were expensive, however, and only the wealthy could afford them.

Although candlemaking was primarily a domestic pursuit during the Middle Ages, the development of medieval towns led to the establishment of candlemakers' guilds whose members, called "chandlers," went from house to house and made candles as required. In France and England two separate guilds were established to distinguish tallow chandlers from wax chandlers.

The earliest American contribution to the history of the candle was made by Colonial women, who discovered that boiling the grayish green berries of the abundantly available bayberry bushes yielded a sweet-smelling wax that burned clean. The process of extracting the wax from the bayberries was so tedious, however, that bayberry candles never gained much popularity.

Toward the end of the eighteenth century the rapid growth of the whaling industry led to the first major change in candlemaking since the Middle Ages. Spermaceti, the wax obtained by crystallizing sperm whale oil, became available for the first time in quantity. This material, like beeswax, did not produce an offensive odor when burned. Another advantage of its use was that it was harder than either tallow or beeswax, and did not soften and bend during the heat of summer.

The first so-called standard candle was made from spermaceti wax. It weighed about three ounces, and was constructed to burn at a uniform rate of 120 grains per hour. The basic unit of light intensity, the candlepower, was based on the light produced by the standard candle.

Most of the major developments which led to contemporary candlemaking occurred in the nineteenth century.

Bronze candlestick in the form of a boy. Italian, 15th century. The Metropolitan Museum of Art. Gift of George Blumenthal, 1941.

21

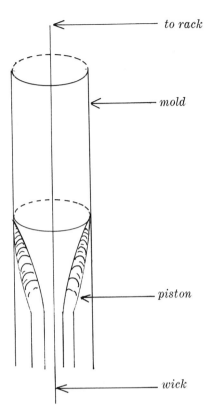

A cross section of a modern candle mold similar to the one Joseph Morgan invented in 1834.

In 1834, Joseph Morgan invented a machine which permitted continuous production of molded candles by use of a cylinder with a movable piston that ejected candles as they hardened. The diagram shows a cross section of a modern candle mold similar to the one Morgan invented.

Modern molding machines contain from 150 to 450 such molds set into a table. Hot wax is poured onto the top of the table, and it flows into all of the molds. Each mold, which is made of highly polished tin, is surrounded by a cold-water jacket. Cold-water treatment enables the hot wax to set in about twenty-five minutes, whereupon a movable piston, shown above, drives up through the mold and ejects the candle, setting it in a rack above the table.

The wicking for the candles is on spindles below the machine. A spool of wick is held under each mold, and wick flows continuously from the spool through the mold, and to the rack holding the finished candle. The candle in the rack above the table holds taut the wick for the candle in the mold. When the wax has set, the wick is cut and the new candle takes its place on the rack, holding the wick in place for the next candle.

One of the country's largest candle manufacturers, the Columbia Wax Products Company, in New York City, makes some 95,000 molded candles *per day* in this manner.

In 1850, a high point in the development of modern candles occurred with the production of paraffin wax from oil and coal shales. By 1859, paraffin was being manufactured by distilling the residues left after crude petroleum was refined. It was discovered that the bluish-white wax burned cleanly, without any unpleasant odor, and was more economical to produce than any candle fuel yet developed.

The one disadvantage of paraffin wax was its relatively low melting point, which made it soften during hot weather. The discovery of stearic acid solved this problem.

During the early part of the eighteenth century, a Frenchman, M. E. Chevreul, found that tallow was composed of fatty acids and glycerin, and that it was glycerin that produced the acrid odor when tallow candles were burned. The fatty acids—stearic and palmitic—burned cleanly and purely. Furthermore, stearic acid was very hard and durable.

By the end of the nineteenth century stearic acid was being produced in quantity and most of the candles being manufactured were composed of paraffin and stearic acid. The result was a hard, clean-burning, odorless candle.

After the invention of the electric light bulb in 1879 candle production in the United States slackened until the turn of the century when a gradual upswing began. The upswing has continued unabated to the present.

During the first half of the twentieth century the growth of America's oil and meat-packing industries contributed to the expansion of candle manufacturing in the United States. As crude oil and meat production increased, so, too, did the by-products that are the basic ingredients of modern candles—paraffin and stearic acid. Thus materials became both plentiful and inexpensive.

The Basics—
How Candles Are Made

There are four basic methods of candle production: dipping, rolling, molding, and extruding. Of these, only extrusion is beyond the capabilities of the home craftsman. Extruded candles are made by forcing wax in powdered or flake form through a shaped opening by applying pressure with a piston, within a mold or cylinder. Some fluted, spiral and cylindrical candles are made by extrusion.

Dipped candles are made by lowering one or more wicks into a container of molten wax, raising the wicks until the wax on them has cooled, then lowering the wicks again long enough for an additional coat of wax to cling to the candle. The process is repeated until a desired thickness is attained.

The shape of candles made by dipping is tapered, being thinnest near the top, and gradually thickening toward the bottom. Thus the name "tapers" is generally applied to such candles. Of the candlemaking methods available to the home craftsman dipping is

Commercially manufactured taper candles. Courtesy Will and Baumer Candle Co.

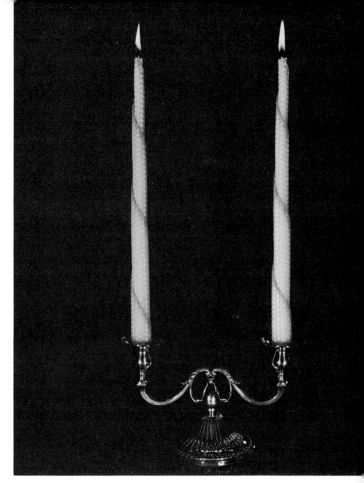

Honeycomb candles. Courtesy A. I. Root Co.

the least popular because of the length of time it takes and the work involved.

Commercially produced tapers are both beautiful and inexpensive, in contrast to home-dipped tapers, which are sometimes irregularly shaped. A section on dipping tapers has been included, because many home craftsmen find the challenge of making tapers stimulating.

Rolled candles are usually made from honeycomb (beeswax) wax which is marketed in thin sheets. Honeycomb wax cannot be used by itself in molds because it is tacky and has very poor mold-release characteristics. Rolling honeycomb wax candles can be a delight and there is virtually no limit to the uses to which the ambitious hobbyist can put this material. A chapter on this very enjoyable form of candlecrafting has been included.

25

By far the most popular form of home candle creation is with the use of molds. This method offers a considerable range of shapes and sizes to the hobbyist, who, once he has learned about molds and mold-making materials, will be limited only by his imagination. It is to molded candles, therefore, that most of the material in this book will be devoted.

WHAT IS A CANDLE AND HOW DOES IT BURN?

In its simplest sense, a candle is a wick surrounded by fuel. Although the fuel can be either liquid or solid, we will consider only solid fuels in this book. The fuel is composed primarily of wax—either paraffin or honeycomb wax plus stearic acid. Paraffin is a petroleum by-product, and honeycomb wax, or beeswax, as it is also known, is an insect wax produced by honey bees during construction of their honeycombs. Stearic acid is one of the components of animal fats.

When a candle is lighted, heat from the match melts the wax in the vicinity of the flame. The melted wax is drawn up the wick by capillary action where heat from the flame evaporates the wax, which then ignites. It is the vapor that burns, not, contrary to popular belief, either the liquid or the solid wax from the candle.

Thus if a candle is to burn properly, there must be a continuous,

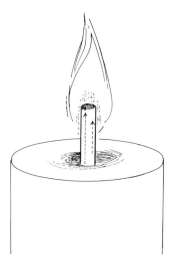

How a candle burns. Liquid wax is drawn up the wick by capillary action. There heat from the flame vaporizes the wax. The vapor ignites, and feeds the flame.

unimpeded flow of melted wax up the wick to the vicinity of the flame, where it vaporizes and continues to feed the flame.

A balance between wick and wax is essential to an efficient, clean-burning candle. Too much or too little liquid wax at the base of the flame, or a wick that is either too large or too small will inhibit good burning qualities in a candle. The result could mean a candle that drips or smokes excessively.

THE FUEL—PARAFFIN WAX

Since the discovery of paraffin wax in 1850, scientists, especially those in the United States, have steadily developed better grades of the material. Paraffin waxes of one hundred years ago had a relatively low melting point, which resulted in candles that wilted and sagged during warm weather, and dripped excessively when burned.

Improved twentieth-century refining methods have paved the way for the production of pure, clean-burning waxes whose melting points range from 128° to 165° F. These waxes have less tendency to drip, and will not wilt as readily during hot weather.

Paraffin wax is a slightly translucent, bluish-white solid at room temperature. When heated to its melting point it becomes a clear, syrupy fluid. When cooled below its melting temperature, it begins to solidify by forming a thin film over the surface that is exposed to air.

As cooling progresses the film thickens, and a depression forms at its center. This depression deepens until the wax is fully cooled, and depending on the shape of the container, could be several inches deep by the time the wax has returned to its solid form.

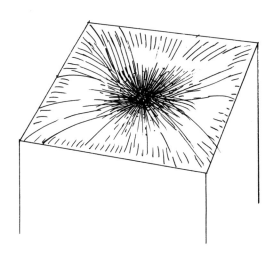

A well will form as paraffin cools. The depression continues to deepen until the wax is fully cooled.

The depression forms because paraffin wax shrinks when it solidifies. This shrinkage can be as much as 10 per cent of the total volume of the wax when it is in liquid form, and is very important to take into account in the making of candles.

Paraffin wax is available in many forms. Some suppliers provide easy to use precut 3/4-pound slabs. It is also supplied in ten- and eleven-pound slabs. These can be broken easily with a hammer, or scored with a penknife and broken along the edge of a table. If a hammer is used to break a wax slab, insert the wax in a burlap bag or an old pillow case to keep wax chips from flying about your work area.

Paraffin supplied by most hobby shops has a melting temperature of approximately 135°F. Some suppliers carry low-, medium-, and high-melting point waxes. These melt at or near 130°, 145°, and 160° respectively. You should know the melting point of the paraffin you purchase.

THE WICK

Most candle-supply shops sell three types of wick—flat-braided, square-braided, and metal-core. Braided wick is made of cotton strands that are braided together. Depending upon how these strands are woven, the wick is either flat or square: Metal-core wick is made by embedding a thin lead filament inside a cotton jacket. The kind of candle being poured determines the type of wick to be used.

Metal-Core Wick

When a candle is burned in a glass container a large pool of liquid wax forms. The wick used in such a candle requires support. Otherwise, it would topple into the liquid and the flame would be extinguished. The lead filament inside the cotton jacket provides the rigidity required for the wick in a glass-container candle.

Candles with a large surface area that form big pools of wax, such as some candles cast in sand, also require metal-core wicks.

Metal-core wicking is made in many sizes, three of which are generally available in hobby shops and candle-supply houses.

These are: small, number 32-24; medium, number 44-24-18, and large, number 44-32-18.

Small metal-core wicks are used in container candles under two inches in diameter, and can also be used in standard candles, such as cylinders and tapers, as well as sand candles under two inches in diameter.

Medium metal-core wicks must be used in container candles having a diameter of from two to four inches, and may also be used in molded and sand-cast candles with a diameter up to four inches.

Large metal-core wicking is required for container candles whose diameter is four inches or more, and in candles whose surface area is large, such as some sand candles; it can also be used in large blocks and cylinders with a diameter greater than four inches.

Braided Wick

Wick without a central filament is made of strands of cotton yarn which are braided together. The number of strands, and the manner in which they are braided, varies.

Braided wick consists of three groups of strands, each group having between four and sixteen strands. The number of strands determines the *ply* of the wick. A wick with six strands per group, for example, is referred to as six-ply wick. Braided wick sold by hobby shops and candle-supply houses averages 27–33 ply.

The groups are braided either flat, as shown below, or square. *Flat-braided* wick curls when burning, and produces a flame that is slightly off center. *Square-braided* wick is woven tighter than the flat, and a cross section is nearly square. It burns with an upright flame.

Flat braided wick. The number of individual strands making up each grouping determines the ply of the wick.

In both square- and flat-braided wicks the tip of the wick is burned off by the flame. Thus the wick is being continually shortened as wax is consumed, and the flame size remains constant.

Flat-braided wick is used primarily in candles having a diameter of two inches or more. If used in smaller candles, the off-center flame heats one side of the candle more than another. This can result in "guttering," in which the side closest to the flame burns down more rapidly than the other, producing a gutter, through which liquid wax drips.

Square-braided wick is used in candles having a diameter less than two inches because the upright flame is a necessity in narrow-diameter candles to minimize dripping. It can also be used in larger-diameter candles.

ADDITIVES

Stearic Acid

Stearic acid, a component of animal fats, is a crystalline substance which, when added to paraffin wax, makes it more opaque, harder, and reduces the tendency to wilt during prolonged exposure to elevated temperatures. Stearic acid does not raise the melting point of the wax when blended with paraffin. It simply makes the wax harder.

There are some instances in which one would not add stearic acid to paraffin. For example, when foliating candles are desired, only paraffin is used. When heated, paraffin splays outward, a requirement in a foliating candle. The addition of stearic acid would inhibit such curling action.

When making chunk candles, which will be covered in greater detail later on, the chunks are embedded in paraffin wax. Because of its translucent quality, more chunks show through. The greater the number of chunks that can be seen, the more effective the candle. If stearic acid were added, the opaqueness of the wax would make it difficult or impossible to see the chunks below the surface. One disadvantage of stearic acid should be mentioned at this point. Over a long period of time, stearic acid in a white candle tends to yellow.

Exactly how much stearic acid to add to paraffin depends on many factors. The type of candle to be made, the color, the melting point of the paraffin you are using, the type and size of the wick, all go into determining the ratio of stearic acid to paraffin. Generally speaking, from 15 to 30 per cent stearic acid by weight, added to the paraffin, will produce a hard, opaque, clean-burning candle. One commercial candle compound containing premixed paraffin and stearic acid uses 20 per cent stearic acid with a 132° F. melting temperature paraffin. I use 25 per cent stearic acid with a similar paraffin.

Polyethelene

Other additives, both natural and synthetic, can be purchased in most candle-supply shops. These either harden or whiten the wax to which they are added. Polyethylene, for example, will make candles glossier, whiter, and harder, but can also clog the wick because it burns more slowly than paraffin when dissolved at temperatures below 200° F. Polyethylene is available under various trade names, but is most frequently referred to as crystals. If used, it should be melted separately, over direct heat, and dissolved in the liquid paraffin. Because of its slower burn rate, a candle to which polyethylene has been added requires a larger-diameter wick than would normally be used to compensate for possible clogging of the wick.

If polyethylene is used, no more than 1 per cent by weight should be added to the paraffin/stearic acid compound.

Beeswax

Beeswax or honeycomb wax is available in two forms—sheets, and slabs; the latter weigh one pound each. Beeswax is a superior material for use in candles because of its clean burning characteristic, high melting point, and elegant appearance. One drawback is that it is three to four times more expensive than paraffin. A second drawback is that it cannot easily be cast in molds because beeswax is extremely tacky, and does not release easily. For these reasons, beeswax is most often used as an additive.

When honeycomb wax is used as an additive to paraffin, it is in the proportion of 30 per cent honeycomb wax to 70 per cent paraffin, or 15 per cent honeycomb wax, 20 per cent stearic acid, and 65 per cent paraffin. The addition of stearic acid improves mold release properties of the candle, and slows its rate of burning.

Pure honeycomb wax candles are made by rolling the sheets into different shapes.

OTHER ADDITIVES

Color

Candle waxes are either white or blue-white in their natural state. They can be colored by adding wax-soluble dyes.

The dyes most commonly used by beginners are crayons. Many of these contain some pigments which are not completely soluble in wax. Consequently there is a tendency for the wick to become clogged, causing a small, smoky flame. Unless crayons are made specifically for candle coloring, they should not be used.

Also to be avoided is food coloring, which is not soluble in wax.

Oil paints are sometimes used for coloring candles, but they are expensive and time-consuming to blend into the wax.

The most satisfactory candle dyes are either in bud, slab, or powder form. The buds or slabs contain heavy concentrations of dye. Small quantities are chipped or shaved off and dissolved in

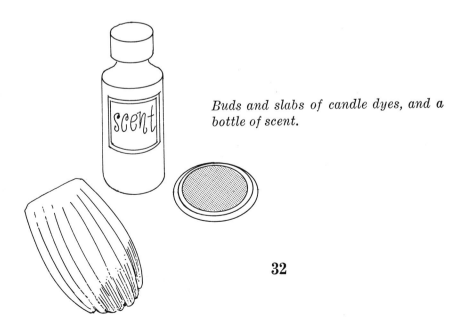

Buds and slabs of candle dyes, and a bottle of scent.

32

melted wax until the desired shade is obtained. The disadvantage of the buds or sticks is that the quantities added to the wax are difficult to measure, and matching colors in pouring successive batches can be a problem.

Dyes in powder form can be measured accurately with a measuring spoon, and once a desired shade is obtained, it can be duplicated by using the same amount of powder. Powder is also more economical to use than buds or slabs.

It is impossible to determine the shade of solid wax you will have from the way it looks in liquid form. Whether you use buds, slabs, or powders, once a quantity of dye has been dissolved in the molten wax, remove a small amount of liquid and put it in a paper hot cup or other container until it solidifies. This process can be speeded up by placing the cup in the freezer. The sample will crack, but no matter; you are primarily interested in determining the color of your wax.

If the hardened wax is lighter than desired, add more dye. If the color is too dark, lighten it by adding more paraffin. Measure the quantities added, if you wish to duplicate the color later on. There are few things more frustrating in candlemaking than having to repeat something you have already done because you forgot how much of each ingredient you used.

Scents

Scents are wax-soluble chemicals which impart a pleasing fragrance to a candle; when it burns, the aroma is released by the flame. Because they do not dissolve in wax, perfumes, colognes, and toilet waters cannot be used. Numerous scents made specifically for use in candles are on the market.

In addition to aesthetics, scents serve a practical purpose. A candle to which citronella has been added, for example, will be helpful in keeping mosquitoes at a distance if burned outdoors.

There are several ways to scent a candle.

The most commonly used method is to add a few drops of liquid scent to the wax before the candle is poured. Four or five drops to a pound of wax is average, although this is a matter of personal preference. It is better initially to use too little, rather than too much, because most scents are suspended in an oil base, and too much oil added to candle wax will result in a mottled candle.

A candle can also be scented by dissolving a small quantity of wax, adding scent to it, then putting precut wicks into this mixture. The wicks are soaked for twenty minutes, giving them ample time to absorb wax and scent. The wicks are then removed, straightened, placed on a piece of wax paper, and when they harden, a batch of prescented wicks is available for use at any time.

Another method of scenting is to add the scent to the well at the base of the flame while the candle is burning. An advantage to this method, if a number of scents are on hand, is that when the few drops that have been added to the candle are consumed, a change of scent can be achieved by using a different fragrance.

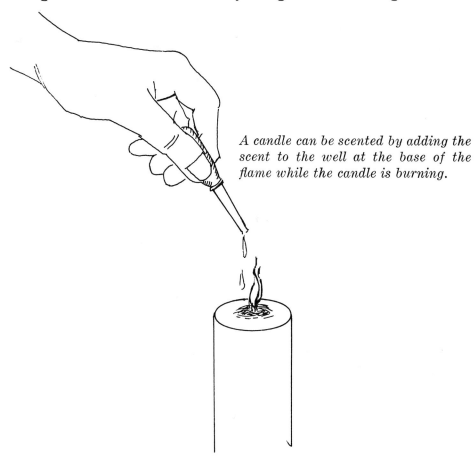

A candle can be scented by adding the scent to the well at the base of the flame while the candle is burning.

GETTING STARTED

The kitchen is an ideal place to work in because it is close to sink and stove. If you have a portable gas or electric stove, or a hot plate, the family room, play room, or basement can be used. Water can be carried in from the kitchen.

Wherever you work, two precautionary steps are recommended: first, use a liberal supply of newspaper to cover your work area and the floor in its vicinty. Wax cannot be poured without dripping, and it is much better to take a few minutes before you start work than to waste precious time later cleaning and scraping wax from difficult-to-get-at areas.

Second, wear washable work clothes. Few craftsmen are so meticulous that they do not sooner or later get wax on their clothing. If this should happen, wait until the wax hardens, then pick off as much as you can. The remainder can be removed by running the affected area under hot water, or by placing paper toweling over the spot and running a moderately hot iron over it.

WHAT YOU WILL NEED

You will need a pot or container for the wax. Since wax ignites at a temperature of approximately 400° F., it is necessary to melt it over boiling water, as in the top of a double boiler. This assures a maximum temperature of 212° for the wax, which is well below its flash point but is at the same time above 200°, the highest temperature you are likely to need. *Never melt wax over direct heat.*

There is one drawback to a double boiler, its capacity is limited, and if you are pouring a large candle, or more than one candle at a time, it may not hold enough wax. Larger containers, such as pitchers, coffee pots, or pails can also be used. In any case, be certain to set the vessel in a pot of water first.

If you melt the wax in a pitcher or other container with a spout, it can be poured directly into the candle mold. Wipe the pitcher with a towel or rag after removing it from the boiling water. Water and wax do not mix, and dripping water into a mold will ruin your candle.

If your melting pot does not have a spout, you can dip a measuring cup into it, and pour from it to the mold.

Wax is a flammable material, and as a precautionary measure a fire extinguisher should be kept on hand at all times. If one is not available and the wax should ignite, the fire can be extinguished by sprinkling baking soda over it, or smothering it with a towel.

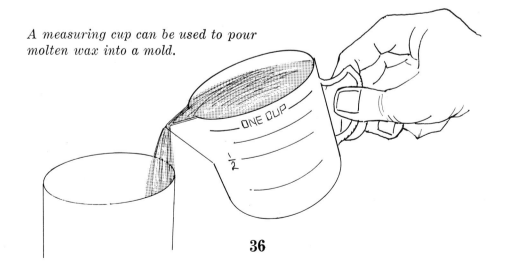

A measuring cup can be used to pour molten wax into a mold.

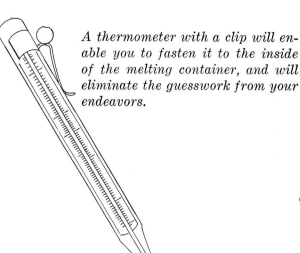

A thermometer with a clip will enable you to fasten it to the inside of the melting container, and will eliminate the guesswork from your endeavors.

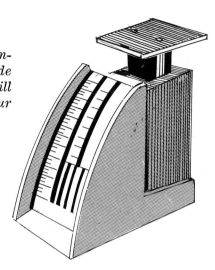

A scale is a necessary piece of equipment for candlecrafters because it will enable you to measure precisely the amount of wax you are melting.

A pot holder is another useful piece of equipment to have on hand when making candles. It is used to grip a hot pot or pail, or a metal mold which has hot wax in it.

Molten wax is usually poured at a temperature ranging from 160° to 195°. A rule of thumb is that the optimum pouring temperature is about 30° above the melting point of the wax you are using. If you continue heating your wax for approximately ten minutes after it is completely melted, the chances are you will be pouring it at the right temperature. Although this method will work fairly well most of the time, a cooking thermometer will eliminate the guesswork from your endeavors. A thermometer with a clip will enable you to fasten the thermometer to the inside of the melting vessel.

A pair of scissors, a pen knife, or a single-edged razor blade should be on hand for cutting wick.

A scale is a necessary piece of equipment for candle craftsmen. It will enable you to measure accurately the amount of wax you are melting, and to add the right amount of stearic acid to your candles. A scale with a two-pound capacity will be adequate for most home candlemaking activities.

USING MOLDS FOUND IN THE KITCHEN

One of the most rewarding aspects of home candlecrafting lies in the use of molds not specifically meant to be used for candles. Because of their appealing shape or availability they lend themselves to candlecrafting. The use of such vessels or containers is limited only by the ingenuity and imagination of the craftsman.

Glass, plastic, rubber, metal, cardboard, and paper containers can be used as molds for candles; if the mold is to be reused, a tapered shape is necessary so the candle will slide out of the mold easily. If the mold is to be used only once, almost any container will do. Once the wax has hardened the mold can be broken, and the candle removed.

Milk cartons, paper cups, cheese, and butter cartons are containers commonly found in the kitchen; all of these can be used as molds for candles.

The walls of such containers are not highly polished, and the candles that such molds produce will not have as high a gloss as those cast in metal, plastic, or rubber. This can be overcome by coating the inside of the container with a thin film of white oil, e.g., cooking or salad oil, and/or by polishing the finished candle with a nylon stocking or soft cloth. In addition, all candles can be veneered with wax or wax decorations, or artificial decorations, such as glitter, paint, etc. These techniques will be discussed later.

Cottage cheese cartons, yogurt containers, and paper cups are among the molds found in the kitchen which can be used to pour candles.

38

MILK-CARTON CANDLE

Let us start by pouring a candle into a mold that is found in most households—the milk carton. After the empty container has been washed and dried, the top half-inch is removed with a sharp knife or razor blade.

The seams that hold the container together are usually sealed with wax, and to ensure against the container springing a leak when hot wax is poured into it, secure the midsection of the carton with masking tape or a rubber band. Wrap tape around the top and bottom of the carton, about one inch from either end, as well.

Next, oil the inside walls of the carton lightly with white oil, which can be applied with a brush, cloth, towel, etc.

INSERTING THE WICK

There are many methods of inserting a wick into a candle. A wick can be inserted either before or after the wax has been poured. It can be secured on the inside, at the bottom of the mold, or it can be hung by weighting one end of it; it can also be fastened outside the mold, through a hole in the bottom. Whichever method is employed, the wick must always be taut and centered in the mold, to assure proper, efficient burning of the candle.

The initial wicking procedure is the same in all instances.

First, cut a piece of wick about two inches longer than the height of the candle. Tie one end of the wick to a stick or pencil. This will serve to suspend the wick at the open end of the mold. Place the stick across the top of the mold, so that the wick hangs down in the center of the mold. The other end of the wick, which

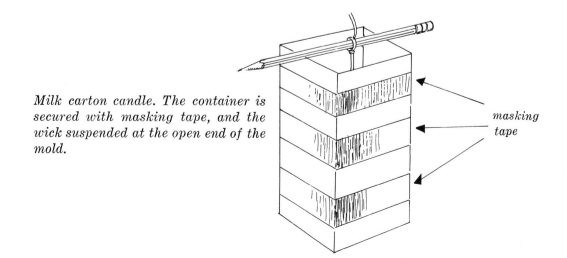

Milk carton candle. The container is secured with masking tape, and the wick suspended at the open end of the mold.

masking tape

will be at the bottom of the candle, and inside it, can be weighted by tying it to a metal nut, washer, or button, and hung so that the weight is suspended just above the bottom of the mold. The weight will keep the wick taut.

An alternate approach is to tack the wick to the bottom of the mold with modeling clay, chewing gum, mold sealer, or any tacky, nonflammable substance that will secure the wick to the bottom of the container.

Still another method of wicking can be used: it is called tacking. The wick is secured to the bottom of the mold with a piece of mold sealer, chewing gum, or clay. It is centered carefully, and a thin layer of molten wax is poured to a depth of about 1/4 inch above the bottom of the mold. The wax is allowed to harden completely, securing the wick in place. With the wick thus "tacked" to the bottom of the mold, it is pulled taut, and fastened to a stick or pencil at the open end of the mold.

A method preferred by some candlecrafters is to first pour the wax into the mold, then lower a weighted wick into it. One advantage to this method is that a minimum of care is needed to keep the wick properly centered while the candle is being poured. Centering, however, remains an important consideration, and care will have to be taken that the pencil or stick holding the wick is adjusted so that the wick is equally distant from all edges of the candle.

For a milk-carton candle, the weighted wick method is recommended.

Before pouring, place the carton into a pot or pan which has been lined with wax paper or aluminum foil. In the unlikely event the container begins to leak, the wax seeping out will be confined to the pan, and the lining will help with the cleanup job afterward.

A milk-container candle can be poured using only paraffin, or a mixture of paraffin and stearic acid. A low-melting-temperature wax is advisable in a milk-container candle because the lower the temperature at which the wax is poured, the less likely it is that the container seams will open. You will need about 2 1/2 pounds of wax to fill a one-quart container.

Whether or not you add stearic acid will depend on the type of candle you desire. An opaque, hard finish will be obtained with stearic acid. A translucent effect results from the use of paraffin only.

Stearic acid can be added to the paraffin either before heating has begun, or after the wax has been melted, or at any intermediate point. Remember one thing: the mix between paraffin and stearic acid is a mechanical one. That is, the two materials do not combine to form one material. They both dissolve, but exist independently in the mixture. Therefore the wax should be stirred thoroughly after melting to get a uniform blend of the materials. Coloring and scents are added when all the wax has melted.

When you are ready to pour, hold the milk carton at a slight angle, and pour wax down the inside wall of the carton. Do not pour into an upright mold because wax falling to the bottom of the container will splash and bubble. Some of the air bubbles will become trapped in the wax, resulting in pit marks when the wax has cooled. Do not pour all the wax at once. Do about two or three inches at a time. This will enable any trapped air in the wax to rise to the surface and escape.

Once the container has been filled to the top, let it sit for half an hour to forty-five minutes. By then the wax will have begun to harden, and a depression will be forming around the wick.

At this point, a hole should be poked in the candle along the wick with a long stick, knitting needle, or piece of wire from a coat hanger to a depth of from one-half to two-thirds the height of the candle. This will prevent cave-ins due to tensions which build up within the candle during the shrinking process.

The well is then filled.

As the candle continues to cool a well will again form, this time not as deep as the first. Once again the depression is filled with wax, which is kept liquid by keeping a small flame under the pot.

It will be necessary to fill a well two or three times, depending on the type of mold being used and the shape of the candle. Candles with a large surface area, such as sand candles, will require fewer pourings, because the depression will form over a wider area and not be as pronounced as the one on a tall, small diameter candle.

When the wax has hardened completely, after six to eight hours, the sides of the carton are peeled away, leaving the candle ready either to burn and enjoy, or to decorate as described later.

INSERTING THE WICK THROUGH A HOLE
IN THE MOLD

When a tapered mold, such as a sour cream or yogurt container is to be used, the finished candle will be more attractive if the narrower end is on top. This requires inserting the wick through the bottom of the mold, so that when the candle is removed and turned upside down, there is a wick at that end of the candle.

To do this, a hole is punched through the bottom of the carton with an ice pick or nail. Be certain it is in the center of the carton. Wick is fed through the hole from the bottom of the mold, and pulled through to the top. The hole is sealed on the outside of the mold with modeling clay, mold sealer, chewing gum, etc., and the other end is tied to a pencil or an ice cream stick. By cutting notches at opposite ends of the opening of the mold, a channel is formed in which the pencil can rest without rolling.

Molten wax is poured into the mold, and bubbling is prevented by pausing frequently as the mold is filled.

When the wax has hardened, the sealer at the bottom of the mold is scraped away, and the candle removed by tapping the open end of the container gently on newspaper or a wooden block. The wick at the bottom of the mold comes through the hole easily. The wick at both ends of the candle is trimmed. Leave about half an inch of wick at the top of the candle.

The same procedures as outlined above can be followed with paper cups, butter containers, plastic cartons, gelatin molds, cookie and muffin tins, etc.

Special cases require special consideration, however. For example, if a conical paper cup is used as a mold, there will be the problem of supporting the pointed bottom of the cup, as shown opposite. You can kill two birds with one stone by using a little ingenuity: An ice pick is used to punch a wick hole at the point of the cup, from inside the cup. The wick is threaded through, and the cup placed into a container with a flat bottom, as shown. Melted wax is poured into the supporting cup, to a level about 1/8 inch above the wick hole. The wax is then allowed to harden. This seals the mold, and provides support for the wick, which is then pulled taut and supported on the rim of the mold with a

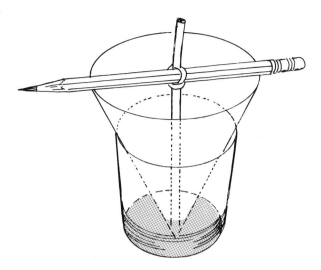

A conical cup is supported by placing it within a flat-bottomed container. About ⅛ inch of wax in the bottom of the outside container will seal the cup and secure the wick.

pencil. The conical cup is then filled slowly with wax. After the wax has hardened, the outer supporting cup is removed and the wax which served to seal the mold is broken off, freeing the wick.

Tin cans are sometimes used as molds for kitchen candles. These are rarely tapered, and a weighted or tacked wick is used in lieu of drilling a hole in the can. Before using a tin can as a mold, make certain there are no ridges or flutes in the wall of the can which could hamper mold release. Many a potentially beautiful candle has been ruined because a candle would not release from a mold.

GLASS MOLDS

Candles cast in glass are simple and rewarding to make. There are three categories of glass-cast candles:

1. The candle is cast with the intention of removing the candle without damaging the mold. This requires a smooth, tapered mold, such as a pilsner glass.

2. The candle is cast in an irregularly shaped glass, which is to be broken to remove the candle. Obviously, such molds can be used only once.

3. The candle is to remain in the glass mold, such as a votive candle. Such molds are refillable when the wax has been consumed.

Unbroken-Mold Candles

Brandy snifters, pilsner glasses, crystal cups and glasses, jars, wine glasses, punch glasses and bowls of various shapes, are among the great variety of glass containers that can be used.

The procedures for pouring candles that are to be removed from glass molds are similar to those outlined for other kitchen candles. The weighted-wick method of insertion is best.

Hot wax can shatter a glass mold. Heating the glass before pouring the wax will prevent such a mishap. Hot water is run over the outside of the glass before the wax is poured. Take care not to wet the inside of the mold.

A wax with a melting point between 130° and 140° F. heated to 160–170° is recommended. If the wax is too cool when it is poured, it will begin to solidify soon after it has been poured, and ripples may form on the inside of the glass, marring the beauty of the candle and making mold release very difficult.

Mold release is facilitated if the inside of the glass is oiled before use. Heating the oil to about 100° saves the step of water-heating the mold.

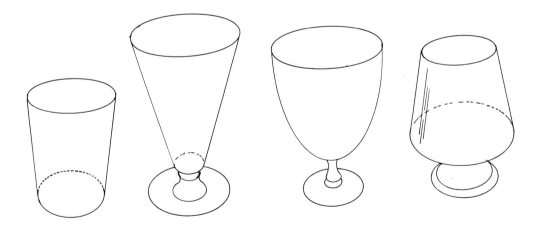

A great variety of glasses can be used for pouring candles.

Broken-Glass Candles

Candles can be removed from inexpensive glass molds by simply breaking the mold after the wax has solidified. There are several safe methods of breaking glass molds, depending on their thickness. One method involves chilling the glass in the freezer for about half an hour, then placing it in a burlap bag or an old towel and immersing it quickly in hot water. The glass can also be broken by wrapping it as above, and tapping it gently with a hammer or other metal object until it cracks. The protective covering is carefully opened, the glass fragments cleared away, and the candle removed.

Wicking and pouring procedures are those already described.

Candles Burned in Their Containers

The simplest of all candles to make are those to be burned in their glass containers because there are no problems of mold release or surface texture.

The most attractive permanent glass containers are either transparent or translucent, not opaque. A candle flame that can be seen flickering through colored and sculptured glass is highly effective.

In making a container candle, there are several important things to remember.

First, *only* wire-core wick is to be used, because this type of candle burns in a pool of liquid wax, and the wick must be able to support itself. If it does not, it will fall over and be extinguished in the liquid wax.

When inserting a wire-core wick hang it from a pencil, allowing about 1/8-inch leeway at the bottom of the container. When hot wax is poured into the mold the wick will expand slightly. If no gap is left at the bottom of the container the expanding wick will buckle.

The container used must be round, and the wick centered carefully, so that heat distribution over the surface of the wax is uniform. This will ensure the formation of a pool of wax over the entire surface of the candle.

Container candles. Courtesy Will and Baumer Candle Co.

Unless there is a pool of wax over the entire surface, the flame will eventually burn down into a well at the center, and unburned wax near the perimeter of the candle will fold over toward the wick and extinguish the flame before all the wax has been consumed.

A low-melting-point wax is used in container candles because of the need for a pool of wax in the container. The higher the melting point of the wax, the larger the flame required to melt all the wax. If the flame is too large, the candle will smoke excessively.

OTHER METHODS OF WICK INSERTION

A wick can be inserted into a candle that has hardened completely by drilling a hole and inserting the wick into the hole. If it is not wire-core wick, it is made rigid by presoaking it in melted wax for several minutes, removing it, and placing it on a piece of wax paper until it hardens.

The prime disadvantage to this method is that most drill bits are relatively short, and the depth of the hole that can be drilled is limited. In addition, unless one is using an electric drill, the procedure is tedious.

When the wick has been inserted, molten wax is poured around it to secure the wick in place.

A similar method of inserting a wick after the candle has hardened requires use of a hot ice pick or a heated piece of wire from a coat hanger to melt a hole in the candle. The wick is inserted and secured with melted wax.

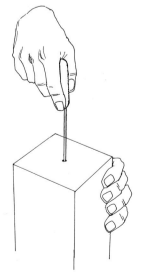

The hot ice pick method of making a wick hole in a candle.

47

The candle-within-a-candle method is also sometimes used to wick a home-crafted candle. In this method, the wax is poured and allowed to begin to form a crust. The crust forms near the walls of the mold, the inside remaining in liquid form the longest. After the crust has formed, a hole is poked in the center of the candle, some of the liquid is poured back into the heating container, and a taper candle that has been cut to the proper length is inserted in the mold. Molten wax is then poured around it, and the well refilled as required when the candle has cooled sufficiently.

CANDLE KITS

The remarkable growth of interest in home candlecrafting has resulted in numerous candlemaking kits reaching the market over the past several years. Many of these are available in arts and crafts shops and five and dime stores. These kits contain all the materials necessary to make decorative candles, including wax, wicking, a melting pot, dye, scent, molds, and instructions. Some contain, in addition, a pot holder, a wick holder, and glitter or other material for decorating the finished candle.

Kits are priced in the range between five and ten dollars and are convenient in that all the materials needed for the beginner to start a candlemaking career are included.

From an economic point of view, however, the cost of the kits generally far exceeds the cost of the materials if they are purchased separately.

Working with Commercial Molds

Once you have created a few candles using molds found in the kitchen you will be eager to move on to bigger and better things. Most hobby and candle-supply outlets now stock a range of molds for making candles that is nothing short of staggering. Scores of molds can be purchased; these are constructed either from metal, plastic, or rubber.

Metal molds are made of tin or tin alloys, and in many different shapes, including cylinders, cubes, pyramids, stars, diamonds, etc. They are highly polished and tapered slightly to assure proper mold release.

RUBBER AND PLASTIC MOLDS

Rubber and plastic molds in the shape of flowers, fruits, animals, figures, filigrees, and a host of other interesting shapes are available at reasonable prices, and most are reusable. These molds

Two-part plastic mold with holder. Courtesy American Handicrafts Co.

50

usually come in two parts, and are fitted together either with clips or holders, into which the molds slide when they are assembled. Casting is the same as with a metal mold, except that in all cases the wax must cool in air rather than water. When the wax has hardened the mold is taken apart, and ridges formed when wax flowed between the parts of the mold are trimmed off with a pen-knife or single-edged blade.

Although various methods of inserting the wick can be used for two-part molded candles, the wick is usually inserted through a hole in the mold. It is secured at the top with a pencil, as in the milk container and other kitchen molds. All commercial molds, whether plastic, rubber, or metal, contain complete instructions for handling the mold and inserting the wick.

Various interesting shapes that can be poured from rubber and plastic molds. Courtesy American Handicrafts Co.

METAL MOLDS

Metal molds must be handled very carefully, since any scratch on the inside of the mold will show on the finished candle. In addition, metals conduct heat more readily than most other materials used in candlemaking, and some extra precautions must therefore be taken while casting candles in metal. Cooling wax may be affected by rapid temperature changes, drafts, non-uniform temperatures over different parts of the mold, etc., and the mold must be protected from these changes while the wax is hardening within it.

A metal mold should never be struck with a hammer or any solid object to facilitate candle release. This can dent the mold or bend the lip, making it useless for further candlemaking. Commercial molds come with a hole at one end for the wick, and are made with an apron at that end so they can stand stably without tipping. In addition, a screw or disc is provided to secure the wick, and to minimize wax seepage through the wick hole.

With these preliminaries taken care of, we are ready to describe the pouring of a candle into a commercially manufactured metal mold:

1. Weigh out the amount of wax you will require for the candle. Most commercial molds will indicate the amount needed. If not, make an estimate. It is better to estimate high and have wax left over, than to be caught short with insufficient wax. This will ruin your candle, because the wax in the mold will begin to solidify before you are able to melt additional wax. If you then add what you were short, the finished candle will show a little line of bubbles, or a streak, where the new hot wax was poured on the cool first batch.

2. Add stearic acid. The formulas for ratio of paraffin to stearic acid are as numerous as the number of candlemakers. No two candlemakers will agree on the exact proportions. In general, 20 per cent stearic acid by weight will produce a fine, opaque, relatively hard candle that will hold color and burn quite well. With experience you will probably alter the formula somewhat, depending on your needs. Possibly you will want a softer candle, or one that drips a bit more. Or perhaps you will want one that is harder

Commercial metal molds. Courtesy Pourette Mfg. Co.

and more opaque, in which case you will use 30 per cent stearic acid. In any event, start with 20 per cent. This means that for eight ounces of paraffin you will add two ounces of stearic acid, for a total of ten ounces of wax.

Place the paraffin and stearic acid in the top of your melting pot.

Dye and scent are added after the wax has melted. The color can be checked by removing a small quantity of wax and letting it cool. You can do this in the freezer, because cracking wax will not be a problem in a test sample. Once you have determined the proportion of dye to use you can return the test samples to the melting pot.

Be careful not to have the water boiling too vigorously, because rapidly boiling water can splash up and get into the wax or into the mold if it is standing nearby.

3. While the paraffin and stearic acid are melting you can put the wick into your mold. Before starting the wicking procedure, make certain the inside of your mold is clean and dry. Dust particles or water inside the mold will mar the candle. A few precautions taken prior to pouring will avoid hours of repeated efforts. Insert the wick into the hole in the bottom of the mold, and feed it through to the top. The wick should be about two inches longer than the mold.

4. Insert the retainer screw or disc into the hole in the bottom of the mold, and screw it tight. This will hold the wick in place. Allow about an inch of wick beyond the screw, and cut the wick at that point.

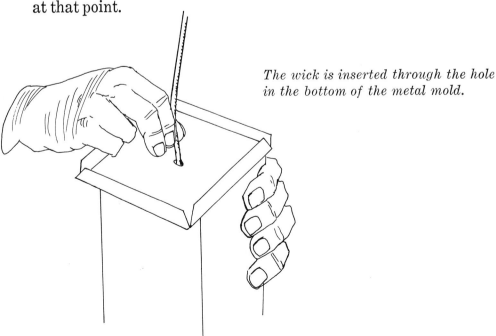

The wick is inserted through the hole in the bottom of the metal mold.

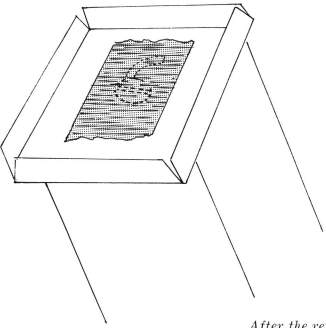

After the retainer screw has been inserted, the bottom of the mold is covered with a piece of masking tape, caulking compound, or mold sealer.

At the open end of the candle tie the wick to a pencil or an ice cream stick, or any object that is larger than the opening of your mold and which will rest stably on the opening. Center the wick and tie it taut.

5. Cover the bottom of the candle, where the screw has been inserted, with masking tape, caulking compound, chewing gum, mold sealer, etc., to prevent leakage through the hole when you begin to pour wax. Actually, if the screw is inserted snugly there is little likelihood of leakage, but initially, at least, this precaution should be taken. If you are planning to insert the mold into a water bath (see below) then it is essential that the screw be covered with a sealer to keep water from leaking into the mold while the wax is still in liquid form.

6. Heat the mold. Pouring hot wax into a cold mold can cause scarring and scaling on the surface of the candle. The mold can be heated in many ways. Standing it on a hot plate, or near the flame of the burner which is being used to melt the wax, will do. Be certain, however, not to place the mold too near the flame, since a temperature of greater than 400° can damage it.

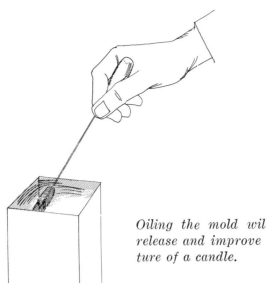

Oiling the mold will promote mold release and improve the surface texture of a candle.

7. Oil the mold. Although this procedure is not mandatory, experience has shown that both mold release and the surface texture of the candle are improved significantly by applying a thin coating of cooking or salad oil to the inner walls of the mold. A basting brush, or any soft cloth mounted on a stick can be used. Be careful not to scratch the inside of the mold while oiling it.

8. When the temperature of the molten wax is 30° F. above the melting point of the wax, you are ready to pour. This assumes the dye has been added and tested satisfactorily. Scent can also be added to the wax at this time. Whether or not scent is used, the wax should be stirred for one to two minutes to make certain the stearic acid is completely mixed in the paraffin.

As mentioned in another section, a scented wick is an alternative to scenting the wax. It is a matter of choice. If the scent is to be added to the wax, however, it is better to use too little initially than too much.

9. With the wick secure and sealed, the mold heated and oiled, the colored and scented wax at the proper temperature, you are now ready for pouring.

Place the mold in a shallow tray or pan, or an aluminum pie plate.

10. Fill your measuring cup about half full of wax, and tilting the mold at an angle while gripping it with a pot holder, start pouring wax gently into the mold on the wall near the top of the

56

opening. The more gradually the wax is poured, the better. Continue pouring wax slowly down the side of the mold until the mold is filled. Pause several times, about fifteen seconds each, to allow any trapped air bubbles to rise to the surface and break.

11. Optional water bath.

If the room in which you are casting your candle is not too cold (65° F. or above) and is relatively draft free, placing the candle in a water bath may not be necessary. Many candlemakers do recommend immersion of the mold in a container of lukewarm water after it has been poured. The mold is immersed to within an inch of the top of the mold. Depending on the height of the mold, any large container can be used for the water bath; a wastepaper basket, an old paint can, a garbage pail, etc.

A water bath is a bother. It takes up valuable space; is cumbersome; requires that a hot mold filled to the top with molten wax be moved, thus increasing the possibility of a minor mishap such as the mold tipping in the water bath, or spilling hot wax on your work area or yourself.

Professional candle manufacturers use water-bath treatments to cool their candles uniformly and quickly. A molded pillar candle, for example, can be cooled in a water bath in some twenty

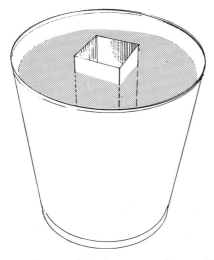

A wastepaper basket can be used to immerse the mold in a bath of lukewarm water.

minutes. But conditions in a factory environment are decidedly different than they are at home, where time is not as important a factor.

Because wax is less dense than an equal amount of water, it will float in water. Depending on the weight of the mold you are using, it may be necessary for you to weight down the mold by placing a heavy object, such as a book, over it, to keep it in the water bath. When the well is to be refilled, and the center opened, (see steps 13 and 14) the weight will have to be removed.

My recommendation is that initially, at least, you try cooling your candle without the use of a water bath. I have rarely used the water bath, and have had good luck, whenever I have taken care to keep the mold out of a draft.

12. Once a crust has formed, and before the well has been filled for the first time, take a dowel, skewer, piece of a wire coat hanger, or knitting needle and poke it into the wax near the wick to a depth of one-half to two-thirds the height of the candle. The stick or dowel should be inserted slowly, so as not to spill wax out over yourself or your work area.

13. When the mold is filled for the first time, the flame under the double boiler is lowered, to keep the remaining wax in liquid form for subsequent filling of the well.

The well is refilled two or three times, at approximately twenty-minute intervals.

14. Cooling. It will take about eight hours for the candle to cool completely. The cooling process can be accelerated by placing the candle in an upright position on the top shelf of your refrigerator. Care will have to be taken not to overcool it. When a mold is cold to the touch it should be removed from the refrigerator. Refrigeration can result in thermal shock. That is, the stresses in the wax that result from too-rapid cooling cause the wax to crack. These cracks, if they do occur, could mar the beauty of your candle.

Placing a candle in the freezer to cool is generally not recommended. But I have placed literally hundreds of candles in the freezer, with only a small percentage cracking under the strain.

15. When the candle has cooled completely, it is ready to remove from the mold. Remove the masking tape or sealer from the bottom of the mold, and take out the screw or disc holding the wick

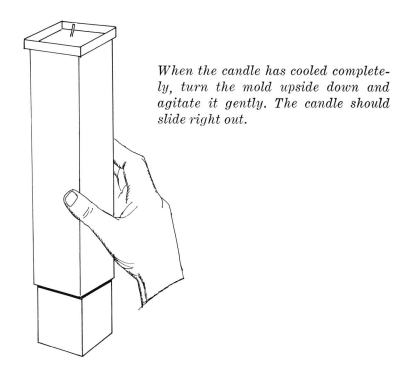

When the candle has cooled completely, turn the mold upside down and agitate it gently. The candle should slide right out.

in the hole. Turn the mold upside down and agitate it gently. The candle should slide right out. If it does not, place some newspapers or folded towels on your work area, and holding the mold open end down, and about three inches above the towels, tap it gently against the papers. This should release the candle. If it does not, it is possible the wax has not cooled enough. Place the mold in the refrigerator for an hour, and try again. That should do it.

If neither refrigeration nor placing the mold in the freezer release the candle it will be necessary to run the mold under hot water. This will mar the surface of the candle, but under the circumstances cannot be prevented.

When the candle has come out of the mold, trim the wick at both ends. The bottom should be trimmed flush with the wax. The wick on top of the candle is trimmed to about half an inch above the surface of the candle.

Some metal molds have a seam on the inside which will appear on your candle. It can be trimmed using any sharp straight-edged instrument, such as a blade, penknife, etc.

The candle is now ready to use and enjoy!!

MAKING YOUR OWN MOLDS

During the past ten years or so, liquid rubbers for making candle molds have been developed. These are useful in casting almost any desired shape into a mold.

One form of liquid rubber sold in hobby shops and through candle-supply outlets is brushed on the model. The coating of rubber is allowed to harden and another coat is applied. Successive coats are added until a durable, flexible mold of the original model has been obtained. When the final coat hardens, the model is removed by pulling the walls of the rubber mold back. The candle mold remaining is hollow, and flexible, and reusable.

Another, more durable, much more expensive material is available in the form of a two-part silicone rubber compound. It is mixed the way most epoxy adhesives are mixed, and it is usable for several hours after mixing, after which it begins to harden. The material hardens fully in twenty-four hours at room temperature, makes extremely durable, extremely faithful reproductions, which can be used hundreds of times without any appreciable deterioration.

One version of this mold-making rubber is manufactured by Dow Corning, Midland, Michigan 48640. Information and details about the material can be obtained by writing the above address, to the attention of Department 165, Moldmaking. The material, called Silastic RTV Liquid Rubber, is of value to anyone interested in reproducing large numbers of candles of an intricate and highly detailed design, such as cut-glass vases and bottles, or sculptures.

Mold making rubbers can also be obtained from the Pourette Manufacturing Company. (See Chapter 12.) All mold-making rubber kits come with complete instructions which are detailed and easy to follow.

Golden cherub, beautiful molded candle, finished by hand. Candles such as this one are made by making a rubber mold from an original sculpture or model. Courtesy Hallmark Cards, Inc.

Three wise men, two-part molded candles. Original works of art can be reproduced in wax by using molding rubber which is available commercially. Courtesy Hallmark Cards, Inc.

Common Problems and How to Cope with Them

In candlecrafting, as in any hobby, things go wrong and problems arise. Fortunately, errors that beginners, or even advanced craftsmen commonly make, are easily correctable.

Most of the problems listed below are also discussed at other points in the body of the text, but are presented here for easy reference.

MOLD RELEASE

One of the most common problems for candlemakers is getting the finished candle out of the mold. There are many possible causes of poor mold release. In the case of metallic molds, it is advisable, after the candle has been removed, to look for damage such as dents in the mold which would hold the candle after it has cooled. If there are no dents, and nothing is found that impedes the release of the candle, it is possible the wax is too soft. Paraffin wax is relatively soft, and the quality and structural characteristics of a candle improve with the addition of stearic acid. Hardening a candle with stearic acid improves its mold-release characteristics because it is less tacky than a candle containing paraffin only.

If wax is not hot enough when poured, it will not shrink as much as it would if its temperature at pouring was about 30° F. above its melting point. Another cause, therefore, of difficult mold release is pouring at too low a temperature.

If too long a time elapses between the first pouring and the second, the well that forms at the top of a candle has a tendency to distort, and the wax may pull away from the side of the mold. When wax is again poured into the mold, some of it seeps down along the wall of the mold where the distortion took place, sometimes forming irregular pockets which hold the candle in the mold. This can be avoided by watching the well carefully and making sure the depression is filled within forty-five minutes of the first pouring.

In the case of nonmetallic molds, the inside surface texture of the mold is often the cause of poor mold release. It is obvious that the smoother the surface of the mold, the more readily the wax will slide over it when it is cooled. Sometimes there are subtle differences in mold diameter which inhibit adequate mold release, and any noncommercial mold should be thoroughly inspected before use the first time.

Silicone sprays are sold at most hobby shops for use with molds to improve release of candles. These sprays form a very thin coating over the mold which promotes easy sliding of the finished candle.

Another method of improving mold release is to coat the inside of the mold with a thin layer of white oil, such as peanut oil or salad oil. The thin film of oil between the wax and the mold promotes mold release.

If a candle will not release, the mold should be placed in the refrigerator for several hours. If, on removal, it will still not release properly, it can be placed in the freezer for an hour or two. If freezing does not help, the candle will have to be ruined by running hot water over the mold and melting some of the wax in it.

Molded candles can be further adorned by hand-painting them using molten wax or acrylic paint in another color. Courtesy Hallmark Cards, Inc.

The skillful use of chunks can result in a dramatically beautiful candle. Courtesy Hallmark Cards.

This molded turtle was hand painted using hot wax as the painting medium. Courtesy Hallmark Cards.

The possibilities of using two-part molds are virtually unlimited. Here a beautiful sculptured rose-like texture makes an exciting candle. Courtesy Hallmark Cards, Inc.

Exciting two-toned effects such as this are possible by applying a coating of white wax over a blue candle, then hand carving a design, or by pouring a thin sheet of white wax into a mold and applying it while it is still soft. Courtesy Hallmark Cards, Inc.

Beautiful Baja scroll candles are available to enhance the home decor.
Courtesy Hallmark Cards, Inc.

Winter candles. Courtesy Emkay Candles, a Rust Craft Subsidiary.

Autumn candles. Courtesy Emkay Candles, a Rust Craft Subsidiary.

Far Left: Decals are used imaginatively on this colorful birthday candle, which is burned down one numeral each year to mark a child's growth.

Left: White candles are used for weddings and anniversaries and can be decorated in many ways. Numerals, wreaths, ribbons, or whipped wax are all appropriate as well as beautiful.

Courtesy Lenox Candles, Inc.

PIT MARKS ON SURFACE OF CANDLE

It sometimes happens that a candle will have small pit marks on its surface when it comes out of a mold. Study of these pit marks will often provide the clue to why it happened. If the pit marks are small and distributed evenly over the entire surface of the candle it is an indication the wax was poured too rapidly into the mold. Rapid pouring agitates the wax, trapping air bubbles inside it. When the candle is removed bubbles appear in the form of little holes in the candle.

Pit marks can also occur if the wax is too cool when poured, shortening the time it takes for it to solidify, or if the mold is too cold when the wax is poured. Wax coming into contact with a cold surface, especially if it is metallic, will harden almost at once, trapping air bubbles before they have a chance to rise to the surface. It is therefore necessary to pour wax at a temperature about 30° above its melting point, and pour it into a warm mold.

Still another cause of pit marks is dust, dirt, or moisture in the mold when the wax is poured. Keep the mold clean at all times, but particularly before pouring.

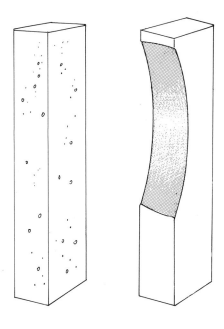

Pit marks (left) can be caused by pouring wax too rapidly, by dust, or by moisture in the mold. Cave-ins (right) are caused by pockets formed within the candle. If these pockets are of sufficient size, forces acting on the outside of the candle will cause one or more walls to buckle. Poking a hole through the well, alongside the wick, will prevent cave-ins.

65

SCALES OR CRACKS ON SURFACE OF CANDLE

Pouring hot wax into a cold mold—especially one of metal—will often result in scales or scars on the candle, particularly near the bottom where the wax first made contact with the mold. Because metal conducts heat rapidly, the hot wax in the bottom of the mold heats up the mold quickly, as a result of which the upper portions of the candle are frequently scar-free, while the bottom is badly marred. Heating a metal mold above room temperature will eliminate scarring. Care should be taken, however, not to heat metal molds much above 400°, because excessive heat could damage the metal or loosen the seals which hold the mold together.

SNOW OR FROST MARKS ON CANDLE SURFACE

These white areas on the surface of candles are minute scars and cracks that occur in a thin outer layer of the candle either because of the presence of moisture in the mold or of temperature differences along the inner face of the mold. All molds should be wiped dry before use, and kept in a dry location when not in use. A thinly applied layer of white oil will also help in reducing snow spots.

The appearance of snow spots does not mean your candle is ruined. Because they are confined to a thin layer at the candle's surface, they can usually be buffed off by using a nylon stocking or a soft cloth, dampened with a light coating of oil. A single-

A single-edged razor blade can be used to clean the surface of a flat candle.

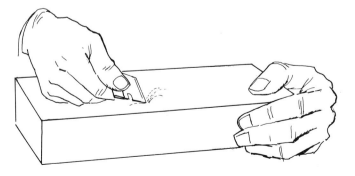

edged razor blade can also be used on flat-surfaced candles to scrape the snow spots off gently. The edge of the blade is held parallel to the surface of the candle, at an angle to it, and is drawn along in the direction of the wick.

EXCESSIVE SMOKING

A properly burning candle represents a balance between the type and size of wick being used, and the quantity and kind of wax being burned. Smoking is due to a deficiency of oxygen in the vicinity of the flame, which results in particles of carbon being carried off in the column of rising gases that surround the flame. The primary cause of smoking is too large a wick. However, the type of wax being used and its melting point are also factors in determining how a candle will burn. A low-melting-point wax, because it can supply more liquid and vapor than the flame can consume, is more apt to smoke than a high-melting-point wax with the same size wick.

There are several possible solutions, therfore, to the problem of a smoking candle: use a smaller wick; use a harder wax, i.e., a higher percentage of stearic acid; use the same size wick in a larger candle.

FLAME TOO SMALL

The wick you are using is too small. A small wick will burn a hole down the center of the candle close to the wick. The hole fills with liquid wax, which eventually diminishes or even extinguishes the flame. A hard, high-melting-point wax can also account for a small flame.

To correct this condition, use a larger wick or a softer wax, i.e., less stearic acid.

DRIPPING

Dripping is caused by a poorly designed candle. A wick that is either too large or too small can cause dripping.

If the wick is too small, it cannot consume all the wax the flame produces; as a result, a pool of wax may form at the base of the wick, and depending on the diameter of the candle, can work its way to the edge of the candle and drip over. Remember, wax expands when it melts, so the volume of wax in liquid form is actually greater than in the solid.

Too large a flame from an oversized wick will melt more wax than the flame can consume, and this, too, can produce a drip, especially if the candle diameter is relatively small.

If wax is too soft it may result in a dripping candle because it liquefies too rapidly. The addition of stearic acid will harden the candle, and lessen the rate at which it melts.

GUTTERING

Sometimes a depression will form along one wall of a candle, and melted wax will run down through this gutter and cause excessive dripping plus uneven burning of the candle.

Guttering can be caused by a wick that is not centered, resulting in greater heat near one edge of the candle than at other edges. It can also be caused by the use of flat-braided wick in a candle that is too thin. Remember, flat-braided wick puts the flame slightly off center. This is all right in a large diameter candle, or in a case where dripping is desired. But if no dripping is wanted, square-braided wick for a small-diameter candle is to be preferred.

SIDES OF THE CANDLE CAVE-IN

It sometimes happens that when a candle is removed from a mold one or more surfaces have a large depression, or cave-in, over part of it.

The forces acting within cooling wax are highly complex, and depend on many factors, including rate of cooling, shape of the mold, type of wax, etc. Frequently, cooling wax will contract internally, especially in the vicinity of the wick, forming a vacuum. If the vacuum is large enough, forces acting on the outside of the candle will push inward from its surface, in the direction of the vacuum, causing the cave-in. See diagram, page 65.

Poking a hole in the candle with a long stick, skewer, or

knitting needle after a well has begun to form will open any vacuum formed inside the candle, eliminating the cause of cave-ins. The well is refilled, as usual, with wax remaining from the first pouring.

SPUTTERING FLAME

Impurities in the wick will cause a flame to sputter. Using crayons to color wax will deposit residues which sometimes accumulate in the wick. There are numerous dyes made specifically for candles, and only these should be used for coloring.

A wet wick will also cause a sputtering flame. Wick that has been lying around near the work area can easily get wet. Keeping the wick in a dry place until it is ready to use is a good practice to follow. Many craftsmen prefer using pre-waxed wicks to avoid such problems.

Wicks of appropriate length are cut and soaked in wax for several minutes. They are then removed and placed on wax paper to dry. The coating of wax protects the wick from air and moisture, and promotes good candle burning. The prewaxed wicks are kept in a cool, dry, convenient location until they are needed.

LINE OF BUBBLES OR CRACKS ENCIRCLES CANDLE

If a partial pouring is made, and the wax allowed to get too cool before another pouring is made, there is likely to be a line of bubbles, or a crack, where the hot wax and the cool made contact.

If a water bath is used, and the water is not deep enough, a line of cracks and bubbles caused by temperature discontinuities could appear along the junction between water and air.

CANDLE BECOMES DIRTY OR SOILED

If a candle you have becomes soiled, it is possible to clean it in several ways. The simplest of these is to wash it with cool water using a mild soap and a sponge or soft cloth. An alternative is to gently dab the candle with white oil on a sponge, nylon stocking, or soft cloth, then wipe it dry.

FADING

Candle dyes are not colorfast over long periods of time, and all candles eventually fade. If a candle is to be stored—as for example a Christmas candle that is used decoratively only during the Yule season—it should be kept in a cool dark place. Exposure to light promotes fading; so will relatively high temperatures. The latter can cause wilting or sagging as well.

Stearic acid in a white candle will, in time, turn yellow, and there is not much that can be done about it, except to use the candle before this happens.

MOTTLING

Splotches or mottles within the surface of the candle are features that some candlemakers build into a candle for the sake of appearance. Since beauty is subjective, this is perfectly acceptable provided one knows how to control it.

A relatively small quantity of oil, as little as 1/2 of 1 per cent by weight, for example, may cause a candle to mottle. Many candle scents are suspended in an oil solution, and the addition of too much scent may cause mottles.

Insufficient stearic acid can also cause mottling. When stearic acid is used, add at least 10 per cent by weight, and stir it about one minute after it has melted.

FRACTURES

The most common cause of fractures is too rapid cooling; either the room was too cold, the mold was placed in the refrigerator too soon, or the mold was placed in the freezer.

A CLOGGED KITCHEN SINK

Molten wax and drains do not mix. *Never* pour liquid wax into a sink.

Rolling Honeycomb
Wax Candles

Beeswax, or honeycomb wax, is the substance honey bees secrete to make the cells of their comb. For centuries craftsmen have used this wax in their finest candles because of its exceptional burning qualities. In the Middle Ages, candles used in Christian church services were made exclusively of honeycomb wax because it was believed that bees came from Paradise.

Honeycomb wax has poor mold-release qualities because it is very tacky. As a result, pure or high percentage mixtures of this wax can not be molded. A small amount of the wax is sometimes blended in with paraffin to improve the burning quality of a candle, and in some instances molded candles are made by filling a mold with paraffin, allowing the wax to harden for half an hour or so, pouring out the liquid wax still remaining in the mold, and filling it with beeswax. Thus the good mold-release qualities of paraffin are combined with the superior burning qualities of honeycomb wax.

For the most part, however, candles made with honeycomb wax are rolled. The wax is available in thin rectangular sheets, approximately eight-by-sixteen inches in a range of colors, and in one-pound slabs. Only the sheets are used for rolling candles.

There are numerous advantages to working with honeycomb sheets: there is no melting required, no molds, no waiting for liquid wax to harden, and no special tools are necessary. The sheets are easy to cut, roll, and mold by hand, and the shape and variety of candles that can be created is limitless.

The tools needed are few; a cutting tool, such as sharp knife, scissors, or single-edge razor blade; a cutting board, such as a piece of Plexiglas, plywood, or wallboard, an eighteen-inch ruler with a metal edge, and a pencil, will get you started.

Honeycomb wax is easily cut with a sharp tool. It is laid on a flat surface, and with the metal edge of the ruler used as a guide, is scored with the blade or knife.

Curved shapes are obtained by first making a pattern of the shape to be cut, or by lightly tracing the shape directly on the wax with a pencil. A pair of scissors can be used when cutting small shapes from scraps that are left over after a large sheet has been trimmed.

The simplest honeycomb wax candle to make is a cylinder which is constructed by rolling a sheet of honeycomb wax around a wick. This is done by first measuring the length of wick needed for the candle. The wick is laid flush with the edge of the sheet. The top

Rolling a honeycomb wax candle. Courtesy A. I. Root Co.

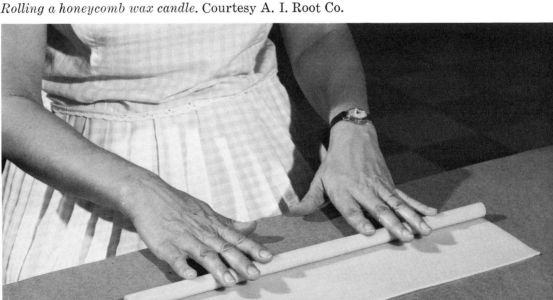

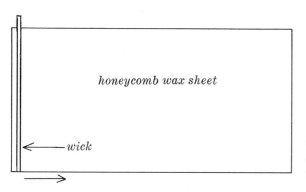

honeycomb wax sheet

wick

Cylindrical honeycomb wax candles are made by rolling the wax around the wick tightly.

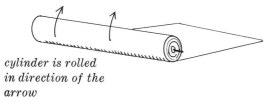

cylinder is rolled
in direction of the
arrow

of the candle will have about half an inch of wick protruding. The wick is then pressed into the sheet. The wax is tacky at room temperatures, and the wick will adhere to it. The edge of the sheet is then rolled around the wick. The first turn is made carefully, rolling the wax tightly against the wick with the fingers. When the wick is surrounded, another tight roll with the fingers is made. Be certain the wax is being rolled straight; the bottom and top edges of the candle should line up. Continue rolling tightly and evenly until the desired thickness is obtained. Using the ruler and the blade, cut the remaining wax off in a line parallel to the wick. The cut edge can then be molded into the candle by applying pressure with the fingers. The warmth of your hands will soften the wax sufficiently for a satisfactory molding job to be done.

For best results, honeycomb wax should be rolled slowly, applying light pressure. The tighter the wax, the better the candle will burn, and the longer. A long piece of wax is rolled by placing the fingers along the edge of the wax and rolling away from you.

Complicated bends can be made by heating the wax in warm water, or on a hot tray. If a hair drier is available, its use is preferred to warm water because it eliminates the necessity of dabbing the wax dry with a paper towel.

The warmer the wax is, the stickier it gets, so some care will have to be taken in working with it at elevated temperatures. There is a tendency to push it too hard when it is tacky and it can tear. Working with the wax is the best way to get the feel of it. It is recommended that until you are familiar with its feel and properties, you do simple candles, such as cylinders, spirals, or layers.

CYLINDERS AND SPHERES

Cylinders can be made in any size or color. A wick of the proper length is laid along the edge of a flat piece of honeycomb wax, and rolled.

The cylinder serves as the basis for other shapes, such as spheres, which can be made by cutting a strip the size of the candle you want and rolling it. A second strip, slightly smaller in width, is added to the first, rolled, and molded into a spherical shape. The number of strips needed to complete the sphere depends on the size of the candle you are rolling.

SPIRALS

Perhaps the most beautiful candles made from honeycomb wax are the graceful, slender spirals made from a piece of wax cut in a triangle with one right angle. The wax is rolled in the direction away from the right angle, as shown. The size of the triangle, and its shape determines whether you have a tall slender candle or a short thicker one.

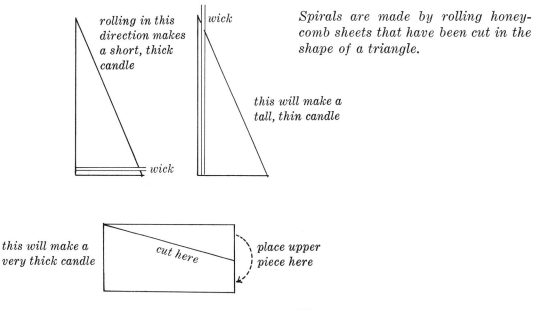

rolling in this direction makes a short, thick candle

wick

wick

Spirals are made by rolling honeycomb sheets that have been cut in the shape of a triangle.

this will make a tall, thin candle

this will make a very thick candle

cut here

place upper piece here

For added length, you can piece the wax as shown in the illustration. As we have said, the tighter the wax is rolled, the longer the candle will burn. Added burning time can be obtained by placing two identical triangles on top of each other, covering them with a piece of wax paper, and rolling them with a rolling pin. The edges must be lined up throughout the rolling.

Once the candle has been rolled, its spiraling edges can be flared or pressed, making the candle conical. This is done by placing the candle on a smooth, flat surface on its side, and rolling it gently with the palm of your hand.

STRIPES

A striped cylinder can be made by cutting strips of different colored wax and laying these side by side, as shown. The strips can be identical in width, or of varying widths. The wick is laid along their edge, and rolled, as with a cylinder. Care is taken to

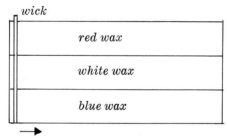

A striped cylinder can be made by cutting strips of different colored wax, laying these side by side, and rolled, as in the case of a cylinder.

keep the strips lined up. The strips should not overlap because that will cause non-uniform thicknesses in the candle.

An alternative and simpler method of rolling a striped candle requires first rolling a small cylinder, then adding the stripes as described above. Each stripe sticks to the cylinder, making unnecessary the more difficult job of tacking the edge of each of the strips to each other.

An unusual candle can be made by rolling triangles of different size that are laid one on the other, with their right angles lined up, and the largest piece on top.

LAYERS

An interesting effect can be obtained by cutting a number of equal-sized squares and laying them one on top of the other until a desired shape is obtained, such as a cube. Before assembly, the pieces are stacked in two equal parts, and a wick inserted. It can be pressed into the wax, or a small niche cut with a razor blade to hold the wick. The two stacks are then placed together with the wick in the center, covered with a piece of wax paper, and pressed together by placing a flat object such as a board, a piece of plastic, a cookie sheet, etc., over the wax paper and applying light pressure.

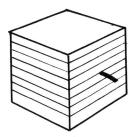

A layered candle can be made by cutting a number of squares of equal size and laying them one on top of the other until a desired shape is obtained.

Different colors of wax can be used for the squares. As an alternative, the layered edges can be covered by cutting a piece that will fit over the square, and pinching the corners and edges together gently. The top of the candle can also be covered by following the same procedure after a small hole has been punched in the center of the square piece. This hole slips over the wick. It can be located accurately by drawing two light diagonal lines along the covering piece. The point at which the lines cross is the center of the cover.

Pieces of the cover can be removed for a decorative effect. Try cutting a circle in the center of the cover before pressing it over the layered square.

Dipping Tapers

Dipped taper candles are made by hanging a number of wicks from a stick, dowel, wire, or any suitable holder and lowering them repeatedly into molten wax until a desired thickness is reached.

Because wax drains toward the bottom of the wick, a gradual thickening of the candle toward its base takes place. This gives rise to the term "taper" applied to all dipped candles.

The wicks are cut to the desired length and prewaxed by soaking them in liquid wax for five minutes, removing them, placing them on a piece of wax paper, and when they are cool, straightening each between the fingers. This is done to assure a smooth, uniform candle.

The wicks are then hung from the dowel at distances of two inches apart. The number of wicks hung depends on the size and shape of the wax container. If six wicks are hung, for example, a container at least 10 1/2 inches wide will be required. It should

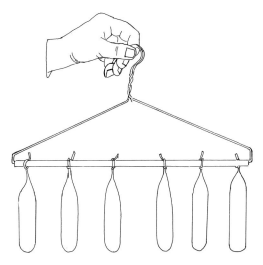

Dipped taper candles are made by hanging a number of wicks from a wire hanger, stick, dowel, etc. and lowering them repeatedly until a desired thickness is reached.

be at least one inch greater in depth than the length of the desired taper. If, for example, a ten-inch candle is to be made, the container should be at least eleven inches high.

The wicking should be either square-braided, if the candle is to be dripless, or flat-braided, if a dripping taper is desired. Small wire-core wick may also be used for a dripless taper.

Wax with a melting point between 130° and 140° F. is heated to 160–170°. Adding about 20 per cent stearic acid to the wax will make a more opaque candle. Opacity is a desirable feature in tapers. In addition, stearic acid reduces dripping.

After the prewaxed wicks have been secured to the wick holder, small weights, such as nuts, shot washers, etc., are tied to the bottom of the wick to keep it straight during the multiple dippings.

Wax on the wicks is built up a layer at a time by dipping the wicks in the wax for about five seconds, then removing them and allowing the wax to harden for two minutes. The cycle is repeated until the candle has been completed.

At normal room temperature, about 70° F., about thirty dips will be required to produce a smooth, opaque taper with a base diameter of a little less than an inch.

Trim the top and bottom of the candle with a sharp knife, leaving about half an inch of wick at the top, and removing the portion with the weight.

Unique Candle Creations

Wax is such an easy material to work with, and is so versatile, that there is literally no limit to the paths the imaginative craftsman can take once he has mastered the basic techniques of candlecrafting.

Many of the candles to be discussed in this chapter are unique in that no two are ever alike. Others are novel, departing from the more or less conventional shapes and forms we have been describing thus far.

A dramatic and exciting innovation in candlecrafting which has captured the imagination of many hobbyists, is the *chunk candle.*

Chunk candles are made by embedding pieces of wax of one or more colors within a molded candle. The chunks at and immediately below the surface of the candle show through, to give a variegated, or marbleized effect which is both beautiful and inter-

A cube-shaped chunk candle.

esting. No two chunk candles are exactly alike because the chunks are put into the mold in a random fashion; in addition, the sizes and shapes of the chunks vary from candle to candle.

The versatility of chunk candles goes even further: any shape and type of mold can be used and the colors of the chunks can be varied in any fashion.

There are also chunk candles in which the chunks literally protrude beyond the surface of the candle.

This multiplicity of possibilities makes the chunk candle one of the most enjoyable to make.

HOW TO MAKE CHUNKS

Chunks are irregularly shaped pieces of wax measuring from 1/4 to two inches across, which are stacked in a mold in a random manner. Molten wax is then poured into the mold. The size of the chunk used will depend on the size of the mold and the effect you are trying to achieve. For a marbleized effect, chunks about one-

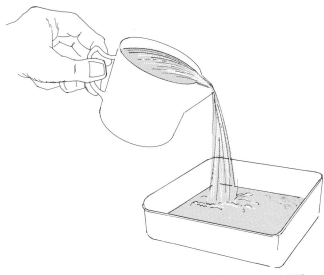

Chunks can be made by pouring molten wax into an aluminum tray. When the wax hardens, the slab is removed and broken.

inch across are desirable. For a mottled effect, smaller pieces are used. And for special effects, larger ones are required.

The simplest way to make chunks is to pour colored molten wax into an aluminum tray. The tins in which frozen foods and baked goods are packed are excellent for this purpose. The pan is first oiled for quick release later, and the wax is poured to a depth of about one inch. A second pouring is unnecessary. When the wax is hard, it is removed by turning the tray upside down and rapping it firmly. If an aluminum tray is used, it can be bent to release the wax. The piece thus obtained can be placed in a bag or sack and broken with a hammer. Or, it can be scored with a knife, and broken by applying pressure at the score line, if more regular shapes are desired. Chunks can also be made in muffin tins, or by using channeling.

Aluminum channeling is available in most hardware and metal supply shops. The channeling can be sealed at either end with masking tape; then liquid wax of the color desired is poured into the channel. When the wax hardens, the masking tape is removed and the bar of wax is removed, and either broken with a hammer and chisel or sawed.

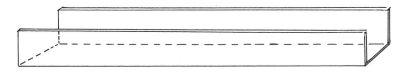

Aluminum channeling can also be used for making chunks.

What Kind of Wax Is Needed

If both a high and a low melting point wax are available, the high temperature wax should be used for the chunks, and the low temperature wax used to pour the candle after the chunks have been placed in the mold. This is done to keep "running" to a minimum. If, for example, a low-temperature wax is used for the chunks, and hot wax is added to these, the chunks will melt and run. The best effects are obtained when the contrast between the chunks and the wax surrounding them is pronounced, and it is therefore desirable to keep melting to a minimum.

The chunks should be made with paraffin plus at least 20 per cent stearic acid. This will inhibit running and will make the chunks more opaque than if only paraffin were used. This opacity will emphasize the contrast between the chunks and the wax in the mold.

The wax poured over the chunks should be paraffin only, without any additives. This is done because paraffin is translucent, and the more chunks that can be seen inside the body of the candle, the more attractive it will be.

Since the use of paraffin alone could make mold release more difficult than if a harder wax were used, it is necessary that the mold be oiled before the chunks are put into it.

The wick is inserted before the chunks are added.

Numerous special effects can be achieved with chunks. The most frequently seen chunk candles are those in which a variety of colors have been placed at random in a mold. But many alternatives are possible. For example, chunks of only one color can be used, such as blue chunks in white paraffin. Several colors can be employed to good advantage. A mold can be filled halfway with red chunks, then blue chunks the rest of the way, with white paraffin poured over them. Any horizontal arrangement of colors can be planned, like blue and green, yellow and orange, etc. Chunks can also be separated vertically. A piece of cardboard can be cut so that it fits diagonally inside a square mold. One side of the mold is filled with chunks of one color, the other side with chunks of a second color. The cardboard is removed, the wick which was inserted prior to the chunks is tied to a wick holder, and the candle poured. White paraffin would be preferable here.

A small supply of chunks should be held aside until after the pouring. There is usually some settling of chunks when the paraffin is poured. Once the settling is over, additional chunks are added.

A striking effect can be achieved by having some of the chunks protrude above the top level of poured wax. This is done by adding chunks after the pouring until they extend above the top of the mold.

Because less melted wax is needed for chunk candles than in other molded candles of equal size, one or two additional pourings of wax to fill the well will be about the maximum required.

The paraffin poured over the chunks is usually white, but can be any color. Pastels are preferred, because the darker the color of the paraffin, the less translucent it will be, and fewer chunks will show through the surface of the candle.

SAND CANDLES

One of the great candle innovations of recent years is the sand candle, which is made by pouring wax into a mold of damp, firmly pressed sand. The result, when it hardens, is a free-form candle in its own container.

Clean sand, fine or coarse, is placed in a shallow container of any size or shape. The sand is dampened. It should be moist, but not wet to the point where water puddles anywhere in the container.

With your hands, or any suitable instrument, such as a wooden spoon, beach shovel, board, etc., form a depression in the sand. This will serve as the mold. It can be round, square, elongated, free form, etc.

Hot wax is poured into the sand mold and allowed to cool. When a well forms, it is refilled. When the wax hardens it is removed, excess sand brushed off, and wicking inserted by using a hot ice-pick, metal coathanger, screwdriver, etc. Wicks can also be inserted by carefully suspending them before pouring. Sticks or pencils can be used by placing them gently on the sand.

The wick should be metal core because the surface area of sand candles is generally fairly large, and pools of wax will form. If the wicking is not self-supporting it will bend over and be extinguished in the liquid wax.

Large sand candles can be made with two or more wicks, and the natural look enhanced with the addition of a piece of driftwood or stone.

The sides of the sand-cast candle can be embellished with stones, shells, jewels, and other decorative materials by embedding them into the sand prior to pouring wax. These should be placed with their most attractive side facing the sand, because these are the sides that will be seen when the wax hardens and comes out of the sand mold.

If the candle is to have legs, they are formed by pressing holes into the sand where the legs are to be. The wax will fill these holes, and form legs when it hardens. If the candle is off balance, it can be leveled by trimming the legs with a pen knife, or placing the candle on a hot tray.

Sand casting is fast. A mold can be formed in the sand in a matter of minutes. The free forms attainable with sand-castings allow a wide range of creative ideas.

If a particular casting is especially attractive, the sand can be removed from the candle with hot water, and the candle cast in a permanent mold, allowing for quantity reproduction of the work.

Similarly, if a casting is not successful, the sand can be washed off, and the wax reused. Nothing lost, experience gained.

The moisture in the sand acts as a barrier to the wax, and the wetter the sand, the less the depth to which the wax will penetrate. The quantity of water added to the sand, therefore, will depend on your requirements. If a layer of sand on the candle is desired, the sand will be dampened slightly; if the sand is to act solely as a mold, it will contain more water, but not to the extent where puddling will occur.

The thickness of the crust can also be controlled by the wax temperature. A hot wax will cool more slowly and have more time to penetrate than one poured at relatively low temperatures. A 130° F. melting point wax, for example, can be poured at 150° for a thin crust, and 160–170° for a thicker crust.

A sand candle with legs.

There is another method for using sand with melted wax to make a container into which wax is poured.

Sand containers are made by blending one part wax at a temperature of about 180° with two parts sand, by volume. Tamp this mixture into a mold, such as a bowl or other vessel whose walls have been oiled for quick release later. When the mixture has hardened, wax of the desired color is poured into the sand container. The wick or wicks can be inserted early by suspending them on a pencil, or inserted later using the hot icepick method.

Only metal-core wick is to be used, unless the surface area of the candle is relatively small.

A mixture of wax and sand was used to make a sand container. After mixture has hardened, wax is poured into the container.

A wax and sand mixture can be used to embellish a molded candle. Here a spoke-shaped candle was enhanced by selective use of waxed sand.

The blend of wax and sand has an exciting rustic texture, which can be combined with wood or other natural materials to produce a piece of sculpture as well as a candle.

Free-form candles can also be made by using aluminum foil set in sand for support. A mold is first made with the heavy-duty aluminum foil available in food stores. It is placed in a bowl or container large enough to hold the mold, and damp sand is firmed around the aluminum foil for support. Oil is brushed on the aluminum foil before wax is poured. Metal-core wick is used.

For added drama, a layered candle can be poured by using different colors, and following the procedures described on page 90 for layering pillar candles.

ICE-CUBE CANDLES

A unique effect can be achieved by pouring a candle into a mold that has been filled with cracked ice or ice cubes. The wax flows around the spaces taken by the cubes, and when it solidifies, the walls of the candle are irregularly shaped, with interesting depressions and holes in them.

Because a candle will not burn properly if the wick is wet, pouring an ice-cube candle requires special wicking procedures:

1. The candle can be poured first, and the wick inserted afterward using a hot icepick or wire coathanger or other long thin implement.

2. A heavily prewaxed wick can be used. To keep the wick as far from water as possible, several coatings of wax are applied to the wick. A method similar to that described in Chapter 7 can be used, or the wicks can be dipped by hand. At least three coats of wax should be applied to the wick before using it in an ice-cube candle.

3. An inexpensive taper candle of the same or similar color as the candle to be poured can be inserted into the center of the mold before adding ice cubes or wax. This is done by pouring about an inch of wax into the mold and waiting for it to begin to solidify. The wax should not be too hard. At room temperature, the wax should begin to gel in about forty minutes. The taper is then centered in the mold. The taper should be about half an inch taller

Ice cube candle (second from left). Courtesy Pourette Mfg. Co.

than the mold, and if necessary, the bottom of the taper can be shortened with a sharp knife before it is set into the mold.

Once the taper is in place at the center of the mold, cracked ice or ice cubes are placed in the mold, and hot wax is poured into it. When the candle is removed from the mold, the taper is trimmed at the top so that it does not protrude above the top of the newly poured candle.

Two things should be remembered in making ice-cube candles. If a commercial metal mold is to be used with a taper wick, be certain to seal the wick hole securely before pouring the bottom inch of wax. Second, after removing the candle, dry the mold thoroughly. Water could ruin a mold by causing it to rust.

In an ice-cube candle it is important to pour the wax at as low a temperature as possible so that it solidifies before the ice melts.

Water sinks to the bottom in liquid wax, and if too much ice melts before the wax hardens, most of the gaps will be at the bottom of the mold.

For this reason, as low a melting point wax as can be obtained, with stearic acid added, is best for use in ice-cube candles.

One method of preventing water from sinking to the bottom of the candle is to pour about one-third of the candle at a time. When wax in the first third of the candle has begun to harden, add more ice cubes and additional molten wax. Again, wait until this wax hardens, then add more cubes. Though this method is somewhat more time-consuming, the results are likely to be better than pouring the entire ice-cube candle at once.

This system enables you to create an interesting effect; you can achieve colored horizontal layers by using a different color for each pouring. A stratified candle with ice-cube holes is thereby obtained.

DICE CANDLES

An interesting novelty candle that resembles a die can be made easily by using honeycomb wax over a square block candle. Square metal molds are available commercially.

Circles are traced on a honeycomb wax sheet, using a coin. The size of the circle will depend on the size of the block being cast. For a four-inch block, e.g., use a nickel. Cut the circles with a blade, linoleum cutter, or penknife, and attach them to the sides and top of the block. Any contrasting colors can be used. The location of the dots can be estimated, using a real die as a model. The circles are positioned first, then are carefully bonded to the candle with a soldering iron with a small tip, a heated knife, etc.

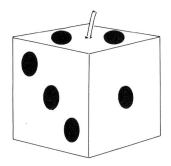

A candle resembling a die can be made by bonding honeycomb wax circles to a square block candle.

89

MULTICOLORED LAYERS

A variety of interesting candles can be made by pouring different colors into a mold, one at a time, with enough time between pourings to allow the wax to solidify. The result is a striped, or layered candle, in two or more colors. The layers can be horizontal, vertical or angled.

Planning is an important part of candle creation, and layered candles require extra preparation. First decide how many colors you want. Next, estimate how much wax you will need in each color. For a candle ten inches tall and three inches square, for example, you will require about three pounds of wax. If you want to pour in three different colors, each layer will be about three and one-third inches high, and will require about one pound of wax.

Prepare your wax and dye in advance, measuring as closely as possible so there will be a minimum of waste. You can also make a layered candle with surplus wax from previous pourings. In any event, the wax you are going to melt down should be at hand.

If you are using a commercial metal mold, the first color you pour will be at the top of the finished candle, since pouring is done with the bottom of the mold facing up.

Melt the first color you want and pour it into the mold. A measuring stick, straight-edge, or ruler which is longer than the mold should be used to determine how much of each color is being poured. To return to the ten-inch mold, for example, you can mark the measuring stick at three and one-third inches, and after inserting the wick, place the measuring stick into the mold and pour your first color until the desired amount of wax is reached.

Once this is done, begin melting your second color. At room temperature, the first pouring will be sufficiently hard in about an hour and you can pour your second color. If you pour too quickly, the hot wax from the second pouring will melt the first pour, and cause "running." The longer you wait between pourings, the sharper the line between colors. If you wait too long, however, the mold may cool to the point where the hot wax will cause some pitting or bubbling at the line between the colors. This is usually not a serious problem in a multicolored stripe, but if you can avoid it, you will have a more nearly perfect candle.

A horizontal striped candle.

By tilting the mold slightly and pouring wax down the side of the mold, splashing, which is a common cause of pit marks in a molded candle, will be kept to a minimum. The measuring stick, which should have been cleaned by scraping off the wax from the first pouring with a penknife, is inserted into the mold, at the wall of the mold, until the bottom touches the first layer of wax. Wax is poured until the mark on the measuring stick is reached. Another method of measuring involves holding the measuring stick at the required distance above the first pouring, and adding the second color until the wax just touches the measuring stick.

Care must be taken, when tilting the mold, to keep the wick properly centered. This can be done by fastening the wick holder to the mold using masking tape, or using a thin piece of flexible aluminum or tin as a wick holder, bending this over the outside of the mold, and securing it with masking tape. The procedure should be followed in pouring angled-layer or vertical-layer candles, as well.

Angled Stripes

The mold is tipped at an angle and supported by a wood block or any object that is large and heavy enough to prop the mold. Successive pourings are made as before. Accurate measurements are more difficult, and the amount of wax to be poured in each color is estimated based on the dimensions of the candle, and the number of colors desired as well as the angles desired.

A great variety of candles can be poured using layering techniques. The angle of the layers can be altered in any manner. For example, the angle of the mold can be reversed with each pouring. A horizontal layer can be alternated with an angled layer, followed by another horizontal layer, and another angled layer at an angle opposite to the first, etc. And of course, the color combinations used with different layers, layer thicknesses, layer angles, etc., are virtually unlimited.

In pouring layered candles, there is a point at which the mold will have to be restored to the vertical position, because wax will run out of the mold after a certain level has been reached. If the final pouring is made using a color that was different from the one

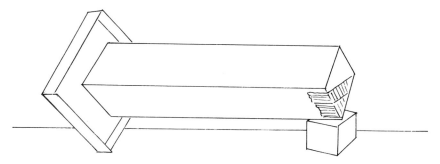

Vetrical layers can be poured by pouring wax into a mold, then resting the candle on its side after masking half the opening.

made when the mold was angled, the illusion of a diagonal stripe will be maintained.

With a little care, vertical-layered candles can be poured by covering half of the open end of the mold with masking tape, pouring wax into the mold, then resting the candle on its side, using a support the same height as the apron at the bottom of the mold. The wax is allowed to harden and, if a two-stripe candle is to be made, the mold is righted, and filled with another color. By pouring less than half the total amount of wax needed, and by changing the position of the masking tape, the candle can be rotated, and various vertical layers poured until the desired effect is achieved.

PETAL-FORMING CANDLES

Some candles with a diameter greater than two inches have edges that curl outward on burning. This splaying, or foliating, is caused by the natural characteristics of low-melting temperature waxes (125–135° F.). These waxes will actually curl away from the source of heat, and if the wick is chosen so that the heat is not great enough to melt the wax at the outer edges of the candle, petal formation will occur. For a three-inch-diameter candle, a flat-braided wick is recommended. It is important that the candle be burned at least three hours at a time to encourage maximum foliation. These candles, also known as angel-wing candles, can be poured in any color, because wax-soluble dyes do not affect the splaying properties of wax.

Pure paraffin is recommended for petal-forming candles.

93

HURRICANE CANDLES

A hurricane candle is one that has been placed within a larger transparent or translucent container. Light from the candle can be seen through the walls of the holder, making an attractive display. Hurricane candles can be used outdoors because the walls of the outer container protect the flame against wind. Any one of innumerable containers available commercially can be used.

Any block or pillar-type candle is suitable for use inside a hurricane container, but for convenience, a candle in a glass jar or vessel should be placed inside the container. This eliminates problems of cleanup from dripping. When the candle has burned down, it is removed, and another put in its place.

HANGING CANDLES

A hanging candle on a porch or patio adds a decorative note to the surroundings.

Low, wide candles, such as a square block or a pillar, are easier to hang because of their stability. Obviously a taper is more difficult to hang than a block.

Many possibilities exist for hanging candles; any base that is wide enough to support the candle can be used. Holes are drilled at opposite ends, and sisal or leather or any suitable material threaded through the holes and knotted at the top. For added interest, the sisal can be macraméd.

Candle-hanging kits are sold commercially, but the creative hobbyist will enjoy making his own hanging arrangement. Make certain the leather or sisal or whatever material is used is far enough from the flame so that it is not heated. A nondrip candle is a must, unless the support for the candle is wide enough, and curved, so that any drippings are caught in the supporting container.

A beautiful petal-formnig candle unfolds as it burns. Courtesy Lenox Candles, Inc.

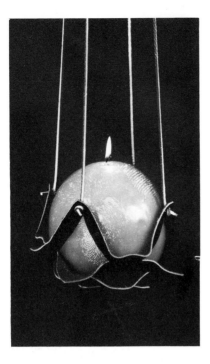

FLOATING CANDLES

A candle will float on water if the surface area of the candle is sufficiently large, and the candle itself is not too heavy. That means a broad, shallow candle such as one cast in a gelatin mold or muffin tin. Flower-shaped molds can be purchased for this purpose.

Floating candles can be used to adorn a fountain or a lily pool, or as part of a centerpiece on the dining table. A crystal or silver bowl filled with water, having several flower candles floating on it, is attractive.

A simple floating candle can be made using a balloon filled with cool water. The balloon is dipped several inches into molten wax for about five seconds, then removed for three minutes. It is then redipped for five seconds more, and again cooled. The process is repeated until a thickness of about one-quarter inch is achieved.

The balloon is drained of water, and the wax shell removed. The edges of the shell can be trimmed and shaped so that it resembles a flower. Slits are cut into it at intervals to enhance the illusion of petals. The shell will float on water. A votive candle can be placed within the shell, and the entire unit set afloat.

A commercial floating candle, and the two-part plastic mold from which it was made. Courtesy American Handicrafts Co.

The Candle as
a Work of Art

Wax can be whipped, sawed, carved, chipped, shaved, veneered, welded, and painted. Decorative materials can be bonded to it. Thus, basic candles can be adorned in many attractive and unusual ways. Though candles are usually for burning, the art of candlecrafting has progressed to the point where a patient craftsman can create a work of beauty which, although it has a wick, does not ultimately have to go up in gentle puffs of smoke. This chapter is devoted to the various methods of decorating candles after they have come out of the mold.

WHIPPING WAX

Wax can be made light and fluffy by whipping it with a beater as one whips cream or egg whites. Billows of puffy white wax can be used to suggest whiskers or snow, and the texture of whipped wax makes it suitable for many interesting candlecrafting effects.

Wax is placed in a container and allowed to cool until a surface film begins to appear. An eggbeater is then used to whip the wax. It become fluffy in a matter of moments, and can be applied to a candle with a fork, spatula, spoon, or any suitable implement. You can even use your fingers provided you wear a rubber glove. The implement you use to apply the wax will depend on the effect you are trying to achieve. A spoon, for example, is useful to give the illusion of snow or billows of clouds. A fork can be used for a textured effect, etc. It will be necessary to whip fresh supplies as the wax in the container is used up. Do not whip too much at one time, because it cools rapidly and becomes difficult to work with.

The area of the candle to which the wax is to be applied can be prepared by brushing it with hot wax immediately before the application of whipped wax. This will improve the bond between the candle and the whipped wax. However, I have applied whipped wax directly to candles without any surface preparation with very good results. Try it that way first. You can always prepare the surface if direct application does not work.

Wax is whipped by allowing it to cool, then beating it until it becomes billowy.

99

Cupcake candle. Cupcake paper was filled with wax, then removed when wax was hardened, and covered with whipped wax. Wick was inserted with a hot ice pick. Cupcake is brown, wax white.

If, for some reason, the whipped wax is not sticking to the candle even after the surface has been prepared with molten wax, it can be bonded by carefully applying a heated icepick or penknife at the contact points and melting the whipped wax and the candle together.

Wax becomes fluffy when whipped because the action of the beater mixes quantities of air into it. The faster the speed at which the wax is whipped, the more billowy it will become. Mixing air with colored wax lightens it, a fact that should be taken into account when colored whipped wax is to be used decoratively.

Sometimes whipping causes lumps to appear in the wax. These can be smoothed out with a heated penknife or icepick, or with a wood-burning tool or soldering iron. (The use of these latter two instruments will be described shortly.) Whipped-wax applications can also be smoothed by dipping the entire candle in a bath of molten wax, either of the same color, or for an interesting effect, a different color.

The candle is gripped securely by the wick with a pair of pliers and immersed for five seconds. For further details, see the section on glazing, below.

Do not expect to make a perfect Santa Claus or snow-covered Christmas tree the first time you try working with whipped wax. It takes a while to get the feel of the process, when to stop whipping, how to apply the wax, how to decorate it. But the rewards to be gained by mastering the technique are manifold, and a little extra time invested with the eggbeater will, in the long run, prove amply satisfying. It is suggested that the first time out you practice whipping uncolored wax and bonding it to a piece of paraffin. This will prevent the waste of wax or a candle.

Clean the eggbeater by allowing the wax on it to harden, then chipping it off. Any residues can be removed by soaking the beater in very hot water.

Chapter 10 offers several suggestions for making candles by using whipped wax.

GLAZING

Most completed candles can be dipped in molten wax to veneer an additional coating of wax, either of another color, or the same color, to repair surface blemishes, or to restore the original color of a candle. This process is called glazing, and it is accomplished by dipping the candle into a pot of liquid wax, keeping it there for five to ten seconds, then removing it quickly. The temperature of the wax should be between 190° and 200° F. The higher the better. There are no particular problems to overcome while glazing a candle, but there is one difficulty in the process itself. If a small candle is to be glazed, a wax melting pot of average size will be sufficient to accomplish the task.

But glazing a ten-inch pillar candle, for example, requires a melting pot at least twelve inches high, and several inches wider than the candle to be glazed. The wider the better, because a candle that is dipped in wax will displace an amount of wax equal to the volume of the candle. Unless a large enough melting pot is used, the wax displaced by the immersed candle is apt to spill over the side of the container.

When dipping the candle it is not advisable to grip the wick in your fingers, unless the wick is an inch or so long. Otherwise, you run the risk of burning your fingertips. A pair of needlenose pliers, gripping the wick firmly, will do the trick. If the wick slips, chances are the candle will be ruined, for by the time it is retrieved some of it will have melted.

WELDING WITH WAX

The "skyscraper" and "rectangular" candles pictured were made by welding bars of wax together with a hot soldering iron, or wood-burning pencil. The mold used was square aluminum tubing cut to various lengths, sealed at one end with 1/8th-inch aluminum sheets cut to 2 x 2-inch squares, and bonded to the aluminum tubing with an epoxy adhesive. To assure mold release, the molds were oiled liberally and heated prior to use. The center element of the skyscraper holds the wick, which is inserted prior to pouring by weighting it with a small nut or washer to keep it centered. The candle can be made in any combination of colors. The central piece is eleven inches tall, and the smallest element is five inches high. The pieces are laid side by side, and the solder-

Skyscraper candles, made by welding wax bars together.

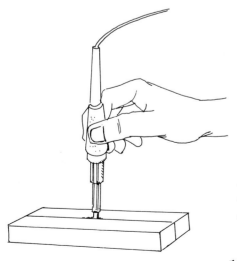

Welding wax. A hot soldering iron or woodburning pencil is used to bond two pieces of wax together by running the iron along their junction.

103

ing iron inserted at one-inch intervals to a depth of half an inch. The wax at the junction between elements melts, and on removal of the iron immediately begins to solidify. When all nine elements have been assembled, the candle is leveled on a hot tray, or with a sharp knife.

The candle is assembled three pieces at a time. The middle section consists of the eleven-inch center, and one nine-inch and one eight-inch piece of another color, on either side. The two outside sections contain one seven-inch piece, and one six-inch and one five-inch piece of the same color as the wicked center. The three sections are then lined up and held together in one hand, while they are welded on the bottom with the soldering iron.

The rectangle is simpler to make. Four pieces of the same size in two colors are assembled by bonding two different colored pieces together. The wick is inserted after running the hot soldering iron the length of the junction between the two pieces and opening a channel large enough to hold the wick. It is placed in the channel and pressed in with the finger. The second two element piece is then bonded to the first by holding the pieces together in one hand and soldering them at the top, near the wick, and at the bottom. The pieces are held in place until the melted wax solidifies, a matter of ten or fifteen seconds, at the most.

The welding techniques described above for the skyscraper candle can be applied in many ways, and sculptured candles of unlimited variety and imagination can be constructed.

VENEERING WITH HONEYCOMB WAX

Honeycomb wax can be applied to a candle with or without the use of heat. Precut shapes can be pinned, cemented with adhesive made especially for candles, or welded with a hot knife or soldering iron.

Honeycomb wax can be cut by using a pair of scissors, a sharp knife, or a razor blade. If the shape to be cut is intricate, a pattern may be required. Otherwise a straight-edge will do the job. Strips of honeycomb wax can be cut and a striped candle made by wrapping strips of different colors around the candle.

Honeycomb wax candles. Striped spirals, and veneered cylinders are shown. Courtesy Pourette Mfg. Co.

DECORATING WITH MOLDED-WAX OBJECTS

Scores of small plastic molds, available commercially, can be used for candle decoration. These shapes range from fruits, birds, flowers, and fish, to shells, figures, crowns, and leaves. Liquid paraffin is poured into the mold and when the wax hardens, the decorations are ready to bond to a candle.

Bonding is accomplished by various means. The back of the piece can be dipped in liquid wax, and when it has softened sufficiently, pressed firmly to the candle to which it is to be bonded. Welding with a wood-burning pencil or soldering iron is another approach, or a hot knife or spoon can be used either to bond the materials or to soften the object to be attached, and pressing it firmly to the candle.

PAINTING ON CANDLES

Painting on a candle with a liquid wax is creative, but some degree of skill and a great deal of patience are required to do it successfully.

Molten wax on a paint brush will cool quickly, and it is imperative that the time delay between dipping and applying the wax to the candle be minimal. In addition, the brush must be dipped after each stroke.

Although it is possible to paint portraits and landscapes with wax, it is advisable that the beginner confine his activities to simple designs, such as flowers, or better still, geometric designs such as squares, circles, diamonds, each in a single color.

The design to be painted can be traced on the candle with a pin, needle, carving tool, or any sharp, pointed instrument. If you are uncertain of your drawing ability, a simple drawing can be traced by placing the drawing on the candle and going over it lightly with a sharp pencil. If the original drawing or design is on thick paper, it will first have to be traced onto onion skin or tissue paper and then transferred by tracing. If you are skilled at draw-

Holly and English holly are bonded to tapers and cylinders using hot wax.
Courtesy Hallmark Cards, Inc.

The eyes of this wise old owl were hand painted. Courtesy Hallmark Cards, Inc.

ing, the design can be drawn directly on the candle with a sharp instrument, but extreme care is dictated since one mistake could ruin a candle.

Round paintbrushes, ranging from size 00 to 2 or 3 can be used for painting; these should be cleaned carefully after each use. When the caked wax is dried, carefully break off the wax, then immerse the brush in boiling water for about a minute. The brush is then dried thoroughly with a towel and returned to its holder.

Because you will not need large quantities of colored wax with which to paint, it is possible to have several colors available in liquid form by using muffin or cupcake tins, to hold the liquid wax. It can be kept hot (a temperature of at least 190° and preferably 200° F. is desirable) by setting the tin in a roasting pan containing boiling water. The water is kept at a boil by a small flame under the roasting pan.

Deeper shades of the same color can be attained by painting additional layers over a design. Two layers of a color will be darker than one, four darker than two, etc.

Once the simple techniques of painting geometrics have been mastered, more difficult designs and drawings can be attempted. Try painting someone's name on a candle, using a different color for each letter. It will make a very nice gift.

In addition to wax, oil and acrylic paints can also be used to paint on candles.

Remember, Rembrandt did not create a masterpiece the first time he held a brush in his hand. Be patient, and the rewards will be ample.

CARVING IN WAX

By using the correct implements, such as wood-carving tools, a sharp knife, a linoleum cutting tool, or even a razor blade, the careful craftsman can create a hand-carved work of art.

Flowers, animals, birds, letters, abstract designs can be carved into candles. Take time at the outset to plan the project carefully, rather than start too soon and ruin the candle. Remember, you only get one chance. Repair work on candle surfaces is seldom successful after a carving error.

Make an outline drawing of the candle on a sheet of onion skin or tissue paper. Draw the shape of the candle to scale. If it is a cylinder, cut the paper so that its edges line up with the top and bottom of the candle, and so that it will extend once around the circumference of the candle. You can do this by securing an edge of the paper to the candle with masking tape, and wrapping the candle in the paper until it covers the entire candle. Mark the place at top and bottom where the paper meets with the first edge. Draw a line joining the marks at top and bottom, cut carefully, and you have a pattern of the candle. You can then make your drawing on the paper. It could be someone's name, or an outline of a bird or animal. Start with something simple. When the drawing on the tissue paper has been completed, place it back on the candle, using masking tape to hold it in place. Trace this pattern onto the candle with a sharp tool. When the tracing paper is removed, an outline of the drawing will have been cut into the surface of the candle.

Carefully carve your drawing into the candle.

There are a number of methods for creating a two-toned effect for carved candles. That is, the candle itself is one color, but just under the surface, where the carving has removed wax, the candle with a different color from the candle as poured. If, for example, you want a red candle with yellow etching, pour a yellow candle and dip it several times in hot red wax. As outlined in the section on glazing, keep the candle immersed five to ten seconds in wax at a temperature of 190° F., and let it cool about three minutes between dippings.

Where a limited area is to be covered with a thin layer of glaze, the wax may be painted on with a brush. Unless great care is taken, however, painting over a large area can result in non-uniformities that are not desirable on a carved candle.

The grooves etched into a candle can also be painted if they are large enough and do not require great accuracy. It is easier to use the glazing method if two-color effects are desired.

WAX FLOWERS

Making wax flowers is time-consuming but highly rewarding. Flowers can be made to decorate candles or into candles themselves. To make petals, pour a thin layer of wax about 1/8th-inch thick onto a cookie sheet or aluminum foil, wait for the wax to solidify, then, while it is still pliable, cut petals with a knife, blade, or other cutting implement, in accordance with a specific pattern or design. The petals are then assembled around a central pattern or design element to form the flower.

There are several methods of keeping the wax pliable, the best of which is the use of an electric hot tray on which a sheet of aluminum foil has been placed. The petals are laid on the warm foil until they are ready to use. If a hot tray is not available the petals can be kept soft by immersing them in water at a temperature of approximately 100°.

In lieu of pouring sheets of wax, honeycomb wax sheets can be used to make flowers. The instructions below for assembling a wax rose are applicable either to sheets of poured wax or to ready-made sheets of honeycomb wax. The advantages of using the latter are pliability at room temperature, ease with which it can be cut with a scissors, and the fact that it can be hand-molded. The color range is greater with poured paraffin; the range of colors available in honeycomb sheets is more limited.

Ultimately, the choice of material for use in making wax flowers will be a matter of personal preference. Both should be tried.

The petals are bonded to each other by pressing them firmly together, or by welding. A hot knife or spoon can be used to bond petals together, but the best welding technique involves the use of either wood-burning pencils or a soldering iron with a long thin tip. The petals are held together and the iron brought into contact with the wax at the point where they join. The iron will quickly melt the wax as it comes into contact with it. No more than 1/16th-inch penetration of the petals with the iron is necessary for a bond.

When the flower has been assembled, it can be bonded to a candle either by dipping its base in molten wax, then quickly bringing it into contact with the candle, or by welding it to the candle. Contact with the iron should be made at all points where flower and candle touch.

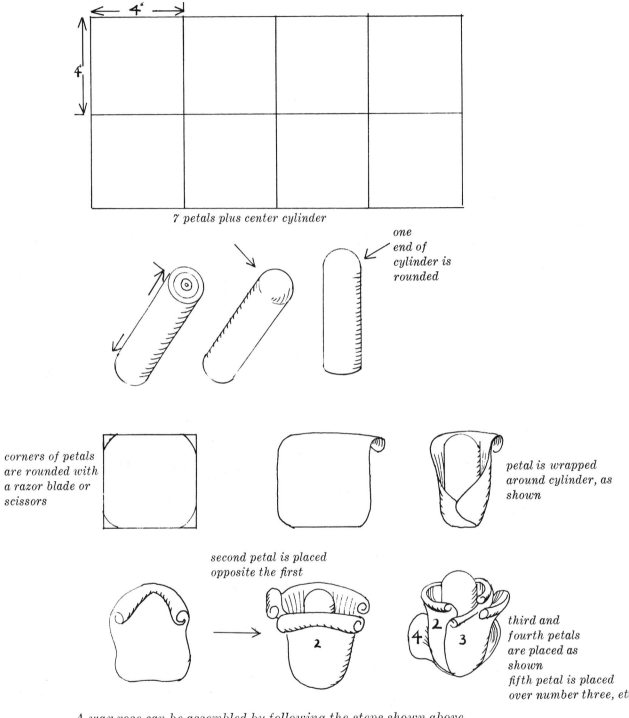

7 petals plus center cylinder

one
end of
cylinder is
rounded

corners of petals
are rounded with
a razor blade or
scissors

petal is wrapped
around cylinder, as
shown

second petal is placed
opposite the first

2

4 2 3

third and
fourth petals
are placed as
shown
fifth petal is placed
over number three, et

A wax rose can be assembled by following the steps shown above.

MOLDED FLOWERS

For the craftsman who is not inclined to spend the time required to assemble his own flowers, a number of flower molds are on the market. These molds are of plastic. Wax is poured into them, and when it hardens a finished flower is the result. Color gradations can be attained by pouring two or more shades of a color into the mold. The first color is poured into part of the candle, and when it begins to set, the second shade is poured. If the first pouring is not permitted to become too hard, the two colors will blend into each other.

GLITTER

Glitter is a decoration that offers endless possibilities for the craftsman. It consists of small particles of aluminum which are available in single colors or mixtures. It is applied to all or part of a candle, and like spangles or sequins, shimmers and "glitters." It is popular for holiday and special-occasion candles.

There are a number of ways to apply glitter to a candle. Most shops that carry glitter also sell glitter cement, an adhesive that is applied to all or part of the candle before the glitter is sprinkled on. Glitter can also be embedded in soft wax; whipped wax is frequently decorated with glitter, and if the material is applied while the whipped wax is still soft and warm it will adhere well. Glitter will also stick to a candle that has been glazed. All or part of the candle is immersed in hot wax, and before the coating of wax has had a chance to solidify, the glitter is applied. It will be partly embedded in the wax and will adhere very well to the candle.

Some oil-based paints which adhere to wax are available commercially, and these are sometimes used to decorate candles. Part of the candle is painted and while the paint is still wet, glitter is applied to it.

Nail polish can also be used to color a candle and it, too, will hold glitter very well. The polish is painted on, and while it is still wet, the glitter is applied.

Stencils can be used to decorate a candle with spray paint, wax, glitter, etc. Courtesy Pourette Mfg. Co.

STENCILS

Stencils for decorating candles can be bought or made. A stencil is a thin sheet of cardboard, metal, or other material into which a design, pattern, letters, etc., have been cut. It can be placed in contact with a candle, and the design or letters painted through it. Stencils can be purchased, or made by tracing a design or word on a piece of cardboard and carefully removing with a razor blade the inside of the letters or design. Paint, wax, or nail polish will

Star-shaped and cylindrical molded candles are covered with whipped wax and given coating of bright gold and silver glitter. Courtesy Hallmark Cards, Inc.

appear on the candle wherever there is an opening in the stencil. The area can then be adorned with glitter for a beautiful effect.

DECALS

Many gift and hobby shops carry a full line of self-adhesive decals. These are purchased with backing which is removed when the decal is ready for application. A wide range of designs is available for all occasions. Some decals will not adhere well to wax. These can be bonded by immersing the candle, with the decal mounted, in a hot-wax bath. A single layer of glaze, made of uncolored paraffin, will provide a protective coating for the decal, without obscuring it.

SEQUINS

Sequins can be applied to candles by embedding them in whipped wax, in a freshly glazed candle, or with pins.

OTHER ARTIFICIAL MATERIALS

Almost anything that is small enough and attractive can be affixed to a candle. This includes artificial fruits, flowers, leaves, costume jewelry, laces, ribbons, trim, fabrics, and photos. These materials can be pinned on, tied, embedded in whipped wax, in glaze, or cemented. Special wax cements are available at many candle-supply and hobby shops. Let your imagination soar.

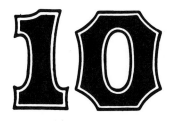

A Candle
for All Seasons

WINTER

Can anyone think of winter without thinking of Christmas? The warmth and joy of the holiday season blend beautifully with the soft glow of candlelight. Is there any wonder the Christmas season evokes the greatest demand for candles as gifts, for decorative purposes, and for the sheer joy of burning them?

A book could be written about Christmas candles alone. The home craftsman can use almost anything to adorn Christmas candles—holly leaves, berries, wreaths, Christmas balls, brightly colored ribbons, to name a few.

A beautiful candle for the occasion is tree-shaped, poured in a bright pine green color, and spotted here and there with white whipped wax to simulate snow. The snow can be decorated with silver glitter, or star-shaped silver sequins, to further enhance

Decals can be used to decorate candles. Courtesy, Lenox Candles, Inc.

A jolly snowman, with red hat, a scarf, and black eyes. Courtesy Hallmark Cards, Inc.

A Christmas candle decorated with Christmas bells and lace. Pictured with the metal mold from which it was cast. Courtesy Pourette Mfg. Co.

Santa, an angel, and a Christmas tree. Courtesy Hallmark Cards, Inc.

the effect of shimmering snow, and the feeling of winter. Tree-shaped molds can be obtained from the Pourette Manufacturing Company. (See Chapter 12.)

Santa Claus molds can be purchased in hobby shops or from candle-supply outlets. The ambitious craftsman can make his own Santa Claus mold with liquid rubber, and decorate the candle with paint and whipped wax. White whipped wax for his beard, of course, red wax for his clothes.

Molded pillar candles can be covered from top to bottom with white whipped wax and sprinkled with glitter and sequins. These molded pillars also lend themselves to adornment with Christmas decorations of all kinds.

The colors of Christmas are red and green, and any mold can be used to make Christmas candles. Pour half in red, the other half in green. Or do alternate stripes, horizontal, or angled.

You can make a red pillar candle and bond a green holly leaf, cut from honeycomb wax sheets, to it.

Or, how about making a stencil in which you have cut the word NOEL, or better still, MERRY CHRISTMAS? The candle can be cast in red, the lettering painted in green. You can, if you are ambitious, carve a Christmas greeting into a candle.

OTHER WINTER CANDLES

Try a round candle, by casting two halves in a mixing bowl. The two halves can be bonded together with hot wax, a soldering iron, or a heated knife. The wick is inserted before the two halves are joined. The ball is then covered with white whipped wax, to simulate a snowball, and can be decorated with glitter, sequins, Christmas balls, or holly leaves and berries, which can be real, artificial, or cut from honeycomb wax. Round molds can also be purchased.

Or, how about a chimney candle? A block candle is cast in white wax, and glazed or overlaid with red wax. A honeycomb overlay can be made to fit over the block candle by bonding a precut piece of smooth honeycomb wax to the white candle. Then, using a sharp knife or wood-working tools, grooves are cut into the red veneer deep enough to have the white show through. The grooves are cut to simulate a brick chimney. White whipped wax is then added to the top and around the bottom of the candle to give the effect of snow.

Strips of honeycomb wax can be cut and assembled to spell HAPPY NEW YEAR. The basic shape used can be a cube, a square, or a columnar type. This lettering can also be painted onto the candle with a mixture of glitter and glitter cement, or it can be carved or painted.

For St. Valentine's Day, heart-shaped molds can be purchased or made from cake pans or candy boxes shaped like a heart. Small heart-shaped molds can be purchased, and the hearts bonded to pillar candles by welding.

For a wintry effect, try casting a blue candle in a metal mold, and after several hours, placing it in the freezer. Leave it for an hour, then remove the mold and the candle. Cracks and fissures will appear below the surface, adding to the illusion of winter. No two candles placed in the freezer will ever come out the same.

How about a snowman candle? Whipped white wax, worked into balls of different size, placed one on the other, and bonded, with painted eyes, nose, and mouth, should get you started on this one. The wick is inserted with a hot icepick before decorating Mr. Snowman.

And for a winter sand candle, use light blue wax in the sand, a twig or small piece of driftwood, adorned with a touch of white whipped wax to simulate snow.

SPRING

The colors of spring are red, orange, yellow, and shades of green, and candles cast in these colors suggest the awakening of life.

When we think of spring, we think of Easter and another awakening. Religious themes on candles require the use of decals, paints, glitter, pictures, or figures. And imagination. Molds with religious themes are available, and in addition religious figures can be cast in rubber. Crosses can be carved, painted, pressed on, stenciled, glittered, or cast separately, then welded on. Flowers can be added to the base of a candle or along its sides for additional decoration.

Eggs are symbols of Easter, too, and egg-shaped candles can be made in several ways. Before molds and mold-making materials became accessible, it was necessary to hollow eggs, dry the shells, then pour wax into the shell to make an egg-shaped candle. Now you can either make your own egg mold or buy egg molds. How

123

Spring candles. Courtesy Gurley
Candle Division, W & F Mfg. Co.
Inc.

you pour and decorate the candles is a matter of personal preference. Pouring stripes, of course, is one very effective method, and adorning them with oil paint, glitter, painting with wax, etc., provides additional means of decorating egg candles.

SUMMER

The motif for summer is flowers. Roses, in particular, are beautiful on candles. Premolded flowers can be added to any pillar candle. You can handcraft flowers too, as previously described. They can be stenciled or painted as well.

The colors of summer are also red, white, and blue, for the Fourth of July. How many possibilities exist there! Try red, white, and blue stripes. Or a red-and-blue chunk candle, with white paraffin. Red-and-blue glitter on a white candle, honeycomb wax stripes in red, and blue stars on a white candle are possibilities.

FALL

The colors of autumn are yellow, orange, brown, gold; the symbols are the turkey, corn, pumpkin, colorful foliage. Halloween is black and orange, with witches, broomsticks, pumpkins, and ghosts. The pumpkin and witches, of course, can be lighted from within, but we are not concerned with anything as commonplace as that. Why not try, instead, to decorate a spherical orange candle to look like a pumpkin! Black eyes, nose, and mouth. Or pour a black-and-orange-striped candle? Cattails and wheat sheafs can be used to adorn fall candles, and turkey molds are available for bonding to candles. How about an orange turkey on a black candle?

Halloween candles. Courtesy Gurley Candle Division, W & F Mfg. Co. Inc.

Autumn candles. Courtesy Gurley Candle Division, W & F Mfg. Co. Inc.

127

Will you be able to deliver? Is the mold you are using available in quantity? Can you get wax and wick at reduced prices? Are your sources of supply reliable? There is more, you must remember, to running a candle business than simply making a beautiful candle.

But don't let the planning aspects of the candle business discourage you. Remember, most successful candle-manufacturing operations started in the home, as a hobby. You can do the same.

Sources of Supply

The growth of the hobby industry during the past generation has resulted in the opening of a large number of hobby-supply outlets throughout the country. Most of these now carry candle-making equipment and materials.

Two major nationwide suppliers are the American Handicrafts Company, of Fort Worth, Texas, and the Pourette Manufacturing Company, Seattle, Washington.

American Handicrafts offers a full line of candle molds, wax, dyes, wick, etc., through the mail. In addition, there are some 200 American Handicrafts stores throughout the country.

A free American Handicrafts catalog can be obtained by writing: The American Handicrafts Company, 1011 Foch Street, Fort Worth, Texas 76107.

The Pourette Manufacturing Company, 6818 Roosevelt Way, N.E., Seattle, Washington 98115, specializes in candlemaking supplies. A catalog can be obtained by writing to the above address, and all materials offered in the catalog can be obtained by mail. The Pourette catalog is $0.35 to cover mailing and handling, and is well worth the cost.

Dyes in powder form and wire-core wick can be obtained by mail from Lumi Craft of Canada, Ltd., RR 3, Box 666 Kingston, Ontario, Canada. Lumi Craft will send a catalog listing dyes and other candle supplies on request.

For the craftsman who wishes to purchase wax in large quantities, The Ross Wax Company, 6–10 Ash Street, Jersey City, New Jersey 07304, offers a complete line of paraffin and stearic acid. These must be purchased in minimum quantities of 100 pounds, with resultant savings for quantity orders.

Index

INDEX